METRO AT 25

METRO AT

25

Celebrating the Past.
Building the Future.

Printed in the United States of America

Washington Metropolitan Area Transit
Authority
    Metro at 25: Celebrating the Past,
Building the Future / WMATA
    Includes index.
ISBN 0-9708719-0-2

Contents

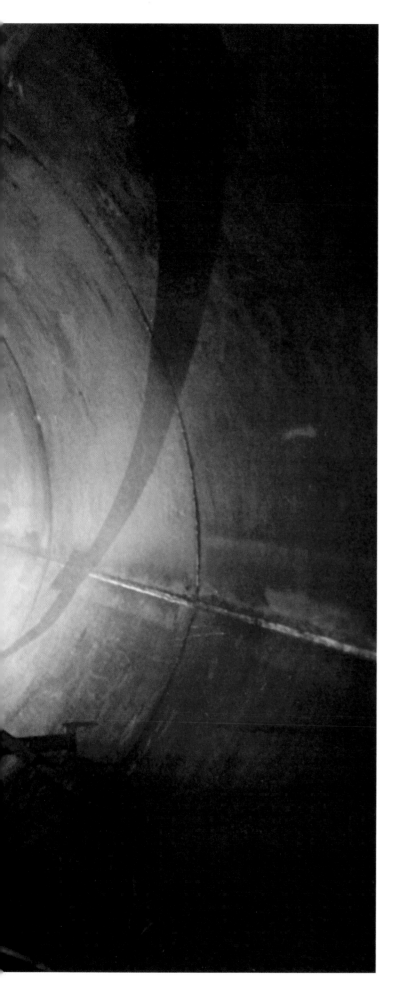

Acknowledgments

This book was produced to commemorate the 25th anniversary of the start of Metrorail rapid transit service in the National Capital Region.

The creative effort was guided by the WMATA Board of Directors' Ad Hoc Committee on the 25th Anniversary:

Cleatus E. Barnett of Maryland
Dana Kauffman of Virginia
Gladys W. Mack of the District of Columbia
Carlton R. Sickles of Maryland

Richard A. White, general manager

This book was written by *R. Wayne Thompson* of the Washington Metropolitan Area Transit Authority. The following Communications staff also participated in its creation:

Leona Agouridis, assistant general manager of
   Communications
Murray C. Bond, director of Strategic Communications
   and Marketing
Marilyn E. Dorfman, manager of Creative Services; art director
   and project coordinator
Gary L. Drake, proofreader
Tom Epps, digital image production
Larry Levine, photographer
Rick Levine, printing specifications
Deborah S. Lipman, director of Government and Community
   Relations
Tim McGowan, digital image production
Phil Portlock, photographer
Paul Willis, principal researcher and Metro archivist

Material for the book was drawn from the following sources:

Metro Memo, Intercom, Metro Weekly and *Inside Metro*
   employee newsletters
Individual biographical files of WMATA's Board of Directors
   and executive staff
Building America's Subway, unpublished manuscript by Booth
   Mooney
Other archival and contemporary material in Metro's files

All photographs and other images in this book were reproduced from Metro's official archive and were taken by Metro's staff photographers and contractors or by agents of Metro's predecessor companies and agencies except where noted.

Cover and page design by Kathleen Sims, Sims Design Co. LLC
Printing by R.R. Donnelley & Sons Co.

Foreword   Carlton R. Sickles

While serving in the Maryland House of Delegates in 1955, I was appointed to the Joint Transportation Commission, an interstate commission established by the District of Columbia, Maryland and Virginia to study passenger carrier facilities in the metropolitan Washington area. Little did I realize, at that time, that I would continue to be involved in related work for the remainder of my professional career. I became a member of the Board of Directors of the interstate compact organization that resulted from our initial deliberations, the Washington Metropolitan Area Transit Authority, and I remain in that capacity today as we celebrate the 25th anniversary of the start of Metrorail service.

The Joint Transportation Commission recommended a three-pronged approach to the problem of providing a coordinated system of transportation in the region. First, it initiated an interstate compact which created an organization to regulate private passenger carrier operations in the region. Second, it recommended legislation to create an interim federal agency that would begin planning for a metropolitan rail rapid transit system. And finally, it negotiated a second interstate compact to establish an organization to complete the plans and build the system.

By the time I entered Congress, I had become chairman of the Joint Transportation Commission, and I continued in that role in addition to my congressional duties. By the end of my second term, the task of the Commission had been completed. The final interstate compact had been adopted by Maryland, Virginia and the District of Columbia, and had been consented to by Congress. The congressional consent process was completed in late 1966, and the legislation creating the Washington Metropolitan Area Transit Authority became effective on February 20, 1967.

Shortly after my second term concluded in January 1967, I was appointed to the Board of Directors of the organization I had helped to create. With two brief interludes in the 1970s, my tenure on that board totals 29 years, and has been uninterrupted in the last 20 years. It has been a labor of love, with opportunity to continue public service to the entire Washington region.

The following pages describe the contributions of the many pioneers who in one way or another contributed to the final result, and without whose help we might still be struggling. It has been my great privilege to know them and to serve along side of them.

The first interstate compact agency recommended by the Joint Transportation Commission was named the Washington Metropolitan Area Transit Commission. It has long since been established, and it still does an outstanding

Carlton R. Sickles is a charter member of the Metro Board of Directors. He also served on the so-called "Shadow Board" that operated just before Metro was created in 1967. As an influential community leader in the 1960s, he chaired the Compact Commission that drafted the transit authority interstate compact.

Mr. Sickles served in the Maryland State Legislature for eight years and as U.S. Representative-at-Large from Maryland in the 88th and 89th Congresses from 1963 to 1967. He is an attorney in private practice and an officer of Carday Associates, a family business.

Mr. Sickles is the second longest-serving member of the Metro Board. He has represented both Montgomery and Prince Georges counties on the Board for a total of 29 years and has served continuously from September 1981 to the present. He distinguished himself as chairman of the Board's Safety and Internal Affairs committees.

Mr. Sickles holds a B.S.S. cum laude from Georgetown University's College of Arts and Sciences and an LL.B. from the Georgetown University School of Law.

job of regulating the private carriers on a regional basis in the area. The interim federal corporation, known as the National Capital Transportation Agency, was created by federal legislation in July 1960, and was dissolved in October 1967 after initiating the planning process and employing a talented technical staff and consulting services, many of which were absorbed by the final compact agency—the Washington Metropolitan Area Transit Authority. It is significant to note that the legislation creating the National Capital Transportation Agency also provided a federal negotiator to work with the Joint Commission to negotiate and draft the transit authority

Finally, one should note that, while the federal government was very much involved in the entire history of the establishment of a Washington subway system, it was determined early on that there would be no federal representation on the transit authority's Board of Directors. It was the specific intent of the founders that Metro not be a federal corporation, but would be owned and controlled by the local governments in the area. Thus, the Metro Board consisted only of local elected officials or their appointees. In spite of this, however, the federal government, recognizing its special responsibility for transportation service in the nation's capital, has in many ways been the major force in bringing about our esteemed, nationally-renowned system, and it has acknowledged its special responsibility to provide funds for its maintenance.

With that background, we are proud to present this pictorial profile of Metro yesterday, today, and tomorrow.

Introduction

The Metrorail system is the product of a unique partnership between the District of Columbia, the State of Maryland and the Commonwealth of Virginia and their respective local governments. The partnership began to take shape with the leadership and cooperation of the federal government in the 1950s during the Eisenhower administration, and it was finally cemented on February 20, 1967 with the passage into law of the Washington Metropolitan Area Transit Authority Compact. The Authority's purpose is to plan, develop, finance and operate improved transit facilities as part of a balanced regional system of transportation.

On December 9, 1969 the Authority broke ground at Judiciary Square in the District of Columbia and began construction of the Metro system, one of the largest single public works projects ever undertaken. On March 27, 1976 the first trains were placed into passenger service on the Red Line between Rhode Island Avenue and Farragut North, and on January 13, 2001 construction of the original system was completed with the opening of the last five stations on the southern end of the Green Line in Prince George's County, Maryland.

The story of the intervening years is one of herculean efforts by the pioneers and visionaries of public transportation in Washington, D.C. It is a story of dramatic setbacks in planning and financing that, at times, left the vision in doubt. It is a story of the give-and-take that leads to a balancing of political interests and resulted in a modern miracle of regionalism and inter-jurisdictional cooperation. And most of all it is a story of extraordinary commitment to purpose by Board members, executive staff and thousands of employees who have dedicated themselves to making the dream of rail rapid transit in Washington come alive.

The residents of Washington, D. C. and its suburbs are rightfully proud of their system, which has been called "America's Subway." It is a product of their effort, too. Repeatedly at the polls the area's residents have affirmed their desire and intention that the Metro be built. They have voted with their feet as well, by riding their system in ever-increasing numbers. The citizens of the nation have likewise expressed their approval of the nation's premier subway by making it a tourist attraction in its own right.

Many of the area's long time residents remember the days when streetcars were king in Washington. They recall the end of streetcar service in 1961, followed by the financial failure of the privately-operated bus system about 12 years later. Those were times of doubt and concern for the future of Washington, as suburban shopping malls and offices attracted economic activity away from downtown. Suburban housing development, construction of hundreds of miles of new streets, parkways and interstate highways, and the age of the automobile seemed to spell doom for public transportation and city centers all across the country.

In spite of the trends, however, the transit pioneers continued to believe in their goal of building a world class rapid transit system in the Nation's Capital; a system befitting the capital of the free world. Leaders stepped forward just when they were needed to keep the vision alive.

As the dream became reality, the Washington Metropolitan Area Transit Authority assembled the most dedicated group of operations professionals to be found anywhere in the country to keep it running. The tone of commitment and dedication set by the early leaders has continued to inspire the workers who have operated Metro's service and maintained its equipment and facilities day after day for the past 25 years.

That same pioneering spirit also inspires today's leaders. Since Metro's plans were first established, land development has moved steadily outward along Washington's suburban arterials, in some cases resulting in the creation of entire fringe cities of significant size. As a result, even though the 103-mile Adopted Regional System is now complete, Metro's pioneering work is far from done. Metro's leaders remain dedicated to fostering redevelopment downtown as well as to serving the growing suburbs and new towns of the area.

Over the years WMATA has taken advantage of pertinent technological developments to keep the system running in top shape and to improve Metro service whenever possible. Developments in credit card and smart card technology have led to a revolution of convenience for Metro's customers in the area of fare collection. Today, over 130,000 Metro customers are using Metro's new SmarTrip card. Many are receiving transit benefits from their employers, who are distributing those benefits via the Internet.

At 25 years of age, Metro has grown and matured into a seasoned operation. It has become an indispensable part of the fabric of everyday life in the Nation's Capital. This book commemorates 25 years of superior service by celebrating the past and by looking forward to building the future. The book is dedicated to those who conceived the Metro system, to those who built it, to those who run it and keep it running, and to the thousands of loyal customers who have made it a success over the past 25 years.

CHAPTER 1

Celebrating the Past

Early History of Transit in Washington

The story of Metro begins before the time of the U.S. Civil War. The first regular route transit service in the Washington area began in 1848 when horse-drawn stagecoach-type vehicles began operating between Georgetown and the Navy Yard via Pennsylvania Avenue and Capitol Hill.

STREET RAILWAYS

In 1862, Congress authorized the construction of the city's first horse-drawn street railway, the Washington & Georgetown, to be operated over the same route, with new service on 7th and 14th streets NW. Other companies quickly followed, and by the end of the 1880s, horsecar lines extended from Boundary Street NW (present-day Florida Avenue) to Anacostia and from Georgetown to 15th and H streets NE.

The world's first successful electrically-powered street railway opened in Richmond, Virginia in 1888. Later that year, when Congress granted a charter to the Eckington & Soldiers' Home Railway, Washington's first electric line was born.

The Washington & Georgetown and the Columbia Railway soon converted their horse-car lines to cable, and beginning in 1890, Washington had cable cars similar to those in San Francisco. When a fire destroyed Washington & Georgetown's power plant in 1897, horses were pressed back into service. Soon both companies powered their lines with electricity.

The turn of the century saw a boom in electric railway construction. Electric cars were cheaper to build and operate and the service they provided was faster and more dependable than other systems. Then, as now, commercial development followed the car lines from downtown. In fact, the street railways were largely responsible for the growth of Washington from a town to a city.

By the start of World War I, with the city's network of trunk lines complete, Washingtonians were riding to work and play on bouncing four-wheel "dinkies." These soon gave way to double-truck cars longer than a modern bus. From special mail cars to the popular open-sided "breezers" that operated in the summer, trolleys of many sizes, shapes and purposes operated throughout the city

FROM STREETCAR TO MOTORBUS

In 1921, the Washington Rapid Transit Co. began operating two bus routes from what is now the Metrobus Northern Division at 14th and Decatur streets NW. The fleet soon grew to 46 buses, including 15 double-deckers, and the era of the motorbus was born.

Starting in the 1920s and moving into the '30s and '40s, local bus companies expanded operations, replacing unprofitable streetcar lines. In 1931, facing considerable expense for track repair on F and G streets in Foggy Bottom, Capital Traction Co. converted to buses. Two years later, Capital Traction and the Washington Railway and Electric Company merged to form Capital Transit Company. Washington Rapid Transit joined the new company in 1936. Over the next three years, major changes to the route network took place as Capital Transit sought to consolidate its operations and eliminate duplicative service.

Buses continued replacing streetcars in 1935 as transit companies tried to make routes more efficient. Even as the streetcar network was shrinking, Capital Transit demonstrated its commitment to continued streetcar service through its support of the Electric Railway Presidents' Conference Committee (PCC). Beginning in 1929, that committee developed the design for what was to become one of the most popular and widely-used vehicles in the history of public transit, commonly known as the PCC car.

Horse-drawn streetcar at 15th and Pennsylvania Avenue NW.

**Capsule
History of
Metro**

More than four decades of planning and building went into creating the transit system that now serves the Nation's Capital. Here are some historical highlights.

1952
July 10 Congress passes National Capital Planning Act mandating preparation of plans for movement of people and goods in the region.

1954
March Maryland and Virginia general assemblies approve joint commission, including representatives from Maryland, Virginia and District of Columbia, to study passenger transportation in Washington area.

Top: A Capital Traction Co. car at the 14th Street and Colorado Avenue terminal.

Bottom: Early electric car and trailer at the Rock Creek loop—the present day Duke Ellington bridge—about 1900.

The first PCC cars were delivered in 1936 and the last in 1952. A few are still in regular route service in Boston, Newark and San Francisco.

In Washington, modern PCC cars were being purchased and more were on order when World War II broke out. Ridership more than doubled between 1940 and 1944, and every streetcar and bus that could run was pressed into service. After the war, transit ridership fell as young families began buying automobiles, and buses resumed replacing streetcars.

A 45-day strike in the summer of 1955 caused Congress to revoke Capital Transit's franchise. A clause in the new franchise required conversion to an all-bus system within seven years. On August 26, 1956, eleven days after takeover, the new company, D.C. Transit System, Inc., implemented a plan to phase out streetcar service. The forced changeover began in earnest in the fall of 1958.when two streetcar lines were converted to bus operations. The last streetcar ran in regular route service in Washington, D.C. on Saturday, January 27, 1962.

From that date until the opening of Metrorail on March 27, 1976, transit service in Washington, D.C. was provided by buses alone. The D.C. Transit System was the main carrier, with other service being provided by three smaller private companies: the Washington Virginia & Maryland Coach Co. operating out of Arlington, Va.; the Alexandria Barcroft & Washington Transit Co. of Alexandria, Va.; and the Washington, Marlboro and Annapolis Motor Lines headquartered in Prince George's County on the District of Columbia - Maryland boundary at Southern Avenue. All four of those companies were purchased by Metro in 1973 to become the nucleus of the Metrobus system.

1959
July 1 Congressionally-funded Mass Transportation Survey presented to President Eisenhower calls for $500 million rapid rail system by 1980.

1960
July 14 President Eisenhower signs National Capital Transportation Act creating National Capital Transportation Agency (NCTA) to develop rapid rail system.

1961
May 4 C. Darwin Stolzenbach confirmed by the U.S. Senate to be administrator of the National Capital Transportation Agency.

1962
November 3 NCTA submits Transit Development Program to President Kennedy proposing an 83-mile, 65-station rapid rail system.

Barney Circle (late 1940s)

Capital Transit Company Bus (1952)

KEY DATES IN METROBUS HISTORY

Feb. 20, 1967 Metro established.

Jan. 14, 1973 Metro buys D.C. Transit, Inc. and WV&M Coach Company for $38.2 million.

Feb. 4, 1973 Metro buys AB&W Transit Company for $10.7 million and WMA Transit Company for $4.5 million, creating the Metrobus system.

July 24, 1974 First Metro bus passenger shelter installed.

Sept. 1, 1974 Last of 620 new AM General buses are placed into service.

June 17, 1979 Forty-three articulated (bend-in-the-middle) buses begin service on Benning Road Line.

July 1, 1979 Metro begins wheelchair lift-equipped service on 12 lines.

Oct. 11, 1982 Metro dedicates newly built Montgomery Division.

Feb. 6, 1989 Newly constructed Landover Division replaces Prince George's Division which is renamed Southern Avenue Annex.

May 16, 1994 Metro begins MetroAccess curb-to-curb service for mobility impaired riders.

June 6, 1995 Prototype of American Ikarus, Metro's newest articulated bus and an American-Hungarian joint venture, debuts at the White House. President Clinton tours the vehicle with Hungarian Prime Minister Gyula Horn.

Oct. 9, 1997 Metro Board approves recommendations of the Regional Mobility Panel to plan, fund and operate Metrobus in a manner similar to Metrorail.

Left: Metro acquires four private bus companies.

1964
March Virginia General Assembly establishes the Northern Virginia Transportation Commission, with members from Arlington and Fairfax counties, and the cities of Alexandria, Falls Church and Fairfax, to plan and develop transportation facilities.

1965
May 4 Maryland Governor J. Millard Tawes signs legislation creating the Washington Suburban Transit District and the Washington Suburban Transit Commission.

May 6 President Johnson designates Walter J. McCarter as NCTA administrator.
September 8 President Johnson signs legislation he had sought authorizing 25-mile, $431 million rapid transit system capable of future expansion.

1966
January 7 De Leuw, Cather & Co. of Chicago engaged as NCTA's general engineering consultant.

CHAPTER 2

The Founders

The Men and Women Who Pioneered

Rail Rapid Transit in Washington

I n 1906 a subway was constructed beneath the U.S. Capitol to carry senators to the Senate Office Building. Three years later, on December 5, 1909, *The Washington Post* published an article titled, "Why Not a Real Subway System for Washington?" While the idea may have been planted in people's minds, the issue remained dormant for another 40 to 50 years.

In 1944 a *Transportation Survey and Plan for the Central Area of Washington, D.C.* was presented to the commissioners of the District of Columbia. It was prepared by J. E. Greiner Co. and De Leuw, Cather & Co. It proposed a 7.1-mile system of subway tunnels through which Washington's streetcars would operate in the downtown area. Its features included multi-level transfer stations, entry mezzanines for fare collection and information, and 300-foot long boarding platforms below the mezzanine level.

In 1954 Maryland, Virginia and the District of Columbia established a Joint Transportation Commission to study the adequacy of passenger carrier facilities and services in the Washington metropolitan area. The Joint Commission was sometimes called the Tri-State Transportation Commission.

In April 1955 Congress approved $500,000 for the National Capital Planning Commission (NCPC) to conduct a "Mass Transportation Survey" of current and future needs in the Washington region. That survey was conducted over the next four years with the cooperation of the Joint Commission. The result was a report published by the Regional Planning Council of the NCPC, titled *A Transportation Plan for the National Capital Region.* It recommended a 33-mile rail rapid transit system to complement the highways that would be built in accordance with the Federal-Aid Highway Act of 1956.

With the exception of the boost in transit ridership prompted by the large influx of people to Washington during World War II, the economics of public transportation had been declining slowly for years. That decline was accelerated following the war. Private transit operators resumed replacing streetcars with buses. Suburban housing ushered in the age of the automobile. The 45-day strike by workers of Capital Transit Company in 1955 sealed the fate of Washington's streetcar system, which ceased operation in 1961.

CREATION OF THE NATIONAL CAPITAL TRANSPORTATION AGENCY

The results of NCPC's Mass Transportation Survey were presented to President Eisenhower on July 1, 1959. The report recommended three things:

1. Rail rapid transit must be provided in the Nation's Capital regardless of the size of the region's highway system.
2. A federal agency should be established to oversee the transportation system in Washington.
3. The District of Columbia, Maryland and Virginia must be brought together into a legal consortium to deal with transportation issues of a regional nature.

Metro reinforces the Lydecker Aqueduct to build the Red Line between Dupont Circle and Woodley Park-Zoo/Adams Morgan.

Following up on those recommendations, U.S. Rep. Joel Broyhill of Virginia introduced a bill to establish the National Capital Transportation Agency (NCTA) as an independent agency of the executive branch, reporting directly to the president. U.S. Sen. Alan Bible of Nevada introduced the same bill in the Senate.

The legislation, the National Capital Transportation Act of 1960, was signed by President Eisenhower on July 14, 1960. It directed NCTA to plan a regional system of highways and mass transit on exclusive rights-of-way, to construct and provide for the operation of regional mass transit facilities and to evaluate the 1959 NCPC transportation plan. The agency was instructed to submit its recommendations to the president no later than November 1, 1962.

As development progressed, there was continuing interest in separating transit from automobile traffic on Washington's downtown streets.

March 10 Harry M. Weese & Associates of Chicago engaged as NCTA's general architectural consultant.

November 6 President Johnson signs bill creating Washington Metropolitan Area Transit Authority (WMATA). Governors of Maryland and Virginia sign November 17 and commissioners of District of Columbia sign November 22.

1967
February 20 WMATA is officially born, coexisting with NCTA for seven months.
March 17 Jackson Graham, Major General USA (Ret.) appointed WMATA's first general manager.
October 1 NCTA expires.

1968
February 9 WMATA Board adopts the name "Metro" for the system.

While the Joint Transportation Commission supported the legislation, they viewed the NCTA as an interim solution only. The Joint Commission favored a three-pronged approach for creating an interstate compact agency controlled by the local governments to own and operate the transit facilities that would be built.

As an interim step, the Joint Commission negotiated the Washington Metropolitan Area Transit Regulation Compact in 1960 to regulate private transit operations in the region. The resulting agency, known as the Washington Metropolitan Area Transit Commission, was the first of the three prongs in the Joint Commission's solution. The Joint Commission allowed that the second prong would be the interim NCTA, permitting the federal government to get things rolling on the construction of new transit facilities while the details of the final interstate compact agency could be negotiated.

In accordance with the National Capital Transportation Act of 1960, the Joint Transportation Commission was delegated the responsibility to negotiate the final interstate compact. A federal negotiator was appointed to assist the commission.

In the meantime, President Eisenhower appointed C&P Telephone executive Holmes Vogel to be NCTA's first administrator. He held the post for only a few months. Following his inauguration in January 1961, President Kennedy appointed C. Darwin Stolzenbach to head the NCTA. His deputy administrator was Warren Quenstedt. Cody Pfanstiehl headed the important NCTA Office of Community Services. These three men, working closely with a small team of experts on the NCTA staff, began to turn the idea of a rail rapid transit system in Washington into a reality.

SELLING AN IDEA

Warren Quenstedt and Cody Pfanstiehl developed a road show to generate public support for rail rapid transit. They had to convince the community that the NCTA's regional transportation plan would be of great benefit to them. Quenstedt and Pfanstiehl also needed to generate support for an interstate compact agency to replace the NCTA, as mandated by the Act.

A native of Pittsburgh, Pa., C. Darwin Stolzenbach came to Washington in 1934 to join the Federal Emergency Relief Administration. For 10 years before coming to NCTA he directed field activities for the Office of Operations Research at Johns Hopkins University.

A native of Norfolk, Va. and a graduate of George Washington University School of Law, Warren D. Quenstedt practiced law in the District of Columbia. He was active in Fairfax County politics, served in the Kennedy-Johnson presidential campaign and as a member of the 1961 Presidential Inaugural Committee.

A native of Illinois, Cody Pfanstiehl started his career as a radio news announcer. He was D.C. press representative for Warner Brothers theaters and worked in promotions for WTOP radio and TV in Washington. He was a promotional manager for the first United Givers Fund campaigns (the predecessor of the United Way) and served on the board of directors. Before his appointment as public affairs director for NCTA, he was a promotion and public relations director for The Washington Evening Star newspaper. He was a member of the board of directors of the Washington Planning and Housing Association.

The NCTA's study, presented to President Kennedy in November 1962 and summarized in a report to Congress in May 1963, was a groundbreaking work. It recommended a substantial freeway network, an improved bus system and the construction of a rail rapid transit system. It was unique in its plan to coordinate trains, buses and automobiles.

March 1 Metro Board unanimously approves 97.2-mile Adopted Regional System (ARS). System includes 38.4 miles in District of Columbia, 29.7 in Maryland and 29.1 in Virginia.

October 1 Original groundbreaking date is postponed pending release of District of Columbia Metro funds. Rep. William Natcher (D-Ky.), who chairs House Subcommittee on Appropriations for District of Columbia, withholds Metro funds in effort to ensure funding for federal highway projects in District of Columbia.

November 5 Voters decisively commit to Metro in Arlington County, Fairfax City, Fairfax County, City of Falls Church and Prince George's County through bond referendums to help finance local shares of Metro costs. Voters say yes by 71.4 percent.

1969
February 7 Metro adopts revised Rapid Rail Plan and Program including relocation of three stations. System grows to nearly 98 miles. By September 29, 1969 all jurisdictions have approved.

Rep. Basil Whitener, a member of the House Committee on the District of Columbia, sponsored the 1963 NCTA funding bill in Congress.

Walter J. McCarter was hailed as the dean of rapid transit in the U.S. He inaugurated rail rapid transit in Cleveland, and was general manager of the Chicago Transit Authority where he combined the elevated and subway systems into a unified whole that included transit bus services. At outlying stations he built automobile parking facilities and he coined the term Kiss-and-Ride to describe the act of a husband being dropped off at a train station by his wife. As general manager in Milwaukee, Mr. McCarter was the first to hire blacks to work as streetcar motormen.

NCTA's proposed rail rapid transit network was 83 miles long and included 65 stations. It would be clean, brightly lit, and would feature air conditioning in the underground stations and on transit vehicles. It would use escalators rather than stairs. The NCTA predicted that system fares would repay construction costs in 40 years.

In June 1963, in response to the NCTA report, representatives Basil Whitener (D-NC) and Joel Broyhill (R-VA) introduced legislation to authorize NCTA to implement the transit portion of its program.

During the ensuing debates on the House floor, Administrator Stolzenbach and the NCTA staff discovered they had angered the highway interests in Congress by proposing a highway system smaller than that set forth in the 1959 NCPC Mass Transit Survey. NCTA was perceived to be "anti-highway." Even some of its most ardent supporters were critical of the way NCTA handled itself. The bill failed to pass and was recommitted to the Committee for further study.

ANOTHER TRY

At the same time, the Joint Transportation Commission, now chaired by Rep. Carlton R. Sickles, continued to pursue completion of its three-pronged approach described earlier. They expected that negotiations to establish an interstate compact agency to replace NCTA would be completed by late 1966. The new agency would assume responsibility for planning, building and operating the proposed rail rapid transit system.

The NCTA, in the meantime, created and issued a new report titled "Rapid Rail Transit for the Nation's Capital,

January 1965." The report proposed a scaled-back 25-mile system costing $461 million. It pointed out that 26 foreign cities (14 national capitals) had rail rapid transit systems in operation or under construction, and that "Washington is practically alone among major capitals of the western world in not having rapid transit." Rather than declining, the systems in older U.S. cities were being modernized and extended. New systems had been built recently in Toronto and Cleveland, and others were proposed for San Francisco, Atlanta and Philadelphia's New Jersey suburbs.

Darwin Stolzenbach resigned from NCTA in 1965. On May 6 he was replaced by Walter J. McCarter, an appointee of President Johnson.

Perceived as a rapid transit expert, Mr. McCarter was effective in lobbying Congress for passage of a new NCTA program bill in the fall of 1965. He never disparaged highways, and always advocated a coordinated system of roads and transit. He met with the American Automobile Association (AAA), one of the groups that had led the opposition to the previous bill. He convinced the highway contractors that rather than being hurt by transit plans, they would be the very companies that would build the rail system.

Again, Rep. Whitener sponsored the necessary legislation to authorize the NCTA's proposed transit development program. Senators Alan Bible of Nevada and Joseph Tydings of Maryland sponsored the Senate versions. In October 1965 funds were finally approved for NCTA to begin work on a rail rapid transit system.

August 9 Council of District of Columbia approves construction of highway projects, meeting a condition of Rep. Natcher for release of District of Columbia Metro funds.

December 9 President Nixon signs bill for federal funding of $1.147 billion over 10-year period.
Metro Board awards the first construction contract for $33.7 million to joint venture of Gordon H. Ball, Inc. of Danville, Ca.; J. F. Shea Co. of Oakland, Ca.; and Norair Engineering Corp. of Washington, D.C. for three-quarter mile segment of cut-and-cover tunnel from 3rd and D streets NW to 10th and G streets NW including Judiciary Sq and Gallery Pl-Chinatown stations.

Metro breaks ground at Judiciary Square with high-ranking federal, state and local officials participating and an estimated audience of 1,500.

Above *left:* Walter McCarter and Darwin Stolzenbach.

Above *center:* The president of AAA Potomac presents Walter McCarter with a golden shovel symbolic of their support of Metro construction.

Above *right:* White House signing ceremony of legislation creating the Washington Metropolitan Area Transit Authority, November 6, 1966.

Below *left:* President Johnson's letter to Walter McCarter upon his appointment to NCTA. President Johnson encourages Mr. McCarter to seek the best from transit systems around the world.

THE WHITE HOUSE
WASHINGTON

February 22, 1966

Dear Mr. McCarter:

The Congress, in enacting the National Capital Transportation Act of 1965, authorized construction of a rail rapid transit system that eventually will be expanded to serve the entire National Capital Region. Transportation is a critical problem for all major urban centers, and what is done here will have significance far beyond this region.

While we seek to resolve problems of moving people and goods within the congested National Capital area, our concerns must not be confined to the utilitarian requirements of transportation alone. We must take this opportunity to make our Capital a more attractive and inspiring place in which to live and work. The Congress has already enacted legislation to assure that beautification is a major consideration in the development of our highway system. The same concern must guide development of plans for mass transit.

In designing the system for the Nation's Capital, I want you to search worldwide for concepts and ideas that can be used to make this system attractive as well as useful. It should be designed so as to set an example for the Nation, and to take its place among the most attractive in the world. In selecting the architects for this system, you must seek those who can best combine utility with good urban design. As you search for the new and innovative, you must also take advantage of the experience of other cities.

I know that your efforts to accomplish these objectives will be of great interest to this community and to other cities faced with the task of coordinating mass transportation facilities with other urban needs. I ask that you report to me periodically on your accomplishments so that we can join in encouraging public discussion of your plans and in taking steps that others may benefit from your experience.

Sincerely,

Honorable Walter J. McCarter
Administrator, National Capital
Transportation Agency
Washington, D. C. 20432

THE BIRTH OF THE METRO COMPACT

One of the last hurdles to be cleared was the creation of a non-federal agency to replace NCTA. That task was taken up by the Joint Transportation Commission. Key leaders in the effort were Virginia state Sen. Charles Fenwick of Arlington, chief representative for Northern Virginia; Carlton R. Sickles representing the interests of Maryland; Robert M. McLaughlin, chairman of the Board of District Commissioners; and Gregory Wolfe, appointed by the president to assist the commission in its negotiations. Attorney Jerome Alper, counsel to the Commission in the negotiations, was the principal author of the compact document.

One of the main drawbacks of the 1963 NCTA bill was the absence of a plan for financing construction of the new system. In connection with its proposal for an interstate compact authority to build the rapid transit system, the Joint Transportation Commission drafted a plan in which the federal government would contribute—along with greater Washington, D.C. area governments—to the construction costs.

In March 1965 the Maryland Legislature authorized Montgomery and Prince George's counties to participate in the proposed compact agency. In May the Washington Suburban Transit Commission was created. The Northern Virginia Transportation Commission (NVTC) was created in March 1964. Its members were Arlington and Fairfax coun-

1970
June 11 Metro Board realigns approximately 2.5 miles of Green Line to improve service for inner city. Rev. Walter Fauntroy, an influential political and community leader and former Metro Board member, was instrumental in bringing about this much-sought-after change in alignment.

1972
May 3 Metro awards $91.6 million contract to Rohr Corp. for first 300 Metrorail cars.
October 21 President Nixon signs bill authorizing the Authority's acquisition of metropolitan area's four privately-owned bus companies.

1973
January 1: Metro buys D.C. Transit, Inc. and WV&M Coach Co. for $38.2 million.

ties and the cities of Alexandria, Fairfax and Falls Church. In February 1966 the Virginia Legislature approved NVTC participation in the interstate compact. Congress held hearings on the compact and the bill was passed in the fall. It was signed by President Johnson on November 6, 1966.

Maryland signed November 11 and Virginia and the District of Columbia signed November 22. The Washington Metropolitan Area Transit Authority (WMATA) was born 90 days later, February 20, 1967, as called for in the statute.

The WMATA Compact established the "transit zone" to include the eight local government jurisdictions shown here.

The Authority is governed by a policy board of six directors consisting of two voting members from each compact signatory: two from the District of Columbia, two from Maryland and two from Virginia. Each jurisdiction also seats two alternates for a total of 12 directors. The Virginia directors are appointed by the Northern Virginia Transportation Commission. The District of Columbia directors are appointed by the Council of the District of Columbia. Two members are representatives of the Mayor and two are members of the City Council. The Washington Suburban Transit Commission (WSTC)

appoints the directors representing Maryland: two each from Montgomery and Prince George's counties. More recently, the Maryland Governor has appointed two members of WSTC who automatically become the two WSTC voting members of the Metro Board.

STARTING TO BUILD

In January 1966, NCTA hired De Leuw, Cather & Co. as its general engineering consultant to create design criteria, system standards, directive drawings and general plans.

In March 1966 NCTA hired the architectural firm of Harry M. Weese & Associates (HWA) as the general architectural consultant to design Metro's physical system. Weese architects immediately researched transit systems around the world for design ideas. In a series of discussions with NCTA, the D.C. Commission of Fine Arts received HWA's proposals warmly. It was unusual—even controversial—to have architects performing a leading role along with engineers in designing a rail transit system. HWA was directly contracted by NCTA rather than subcontracted to the engineers, a more common practice in large public works projects.

In the 90-day interval between the signing of the WMATA legislation and the birth of the agency, a provisional Board of Directors began work. The first official Board of Directors was sworn in February 20, 1967.

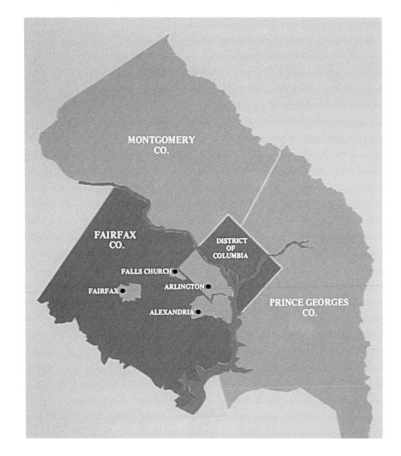

NCTA Administrator Walter McCarter announces the selection of Harry Weese & Associates to be general architectural consultant, March 10, 1966. *Front row, from left:* Harry Weese; Administrator McCarter; Elizabeth Rowe, chair of the National Capital Planning Commission; rear, HWA architect Stan Allen and NCTA Deputy Administrator Robert Reynolds.

February 4 Metro buys AB&W Transit Co. for $10.7 million and WMA Transit Co. for $4.5 million, creating Metrobus system. Metro drops transfer charges, extends senior citizen discounts regionwide, and begins selected fare reductions on routes formerly served by different carriers at different rates. Metro also unifies bus appearance with red, white and blue paint scheme and purchases 620 buses.

August 13 President Nixon signs Federal Aid Highway Act of 1973, authorizing up to $65 million for construction of facilities to make Metrorail accessible for people with disabilities.

August 16 President Nixon signs bill enabling U.S. Department of Transportation to pay Metro $90.4 million for fiscal 1974, $7.5 million covering the design and construction of Arlington Cemetery station and the National Mall entrance to Smithsonian station.

FIRST METRO BOARD OF DIRECTORS

Representing the District of Columbia
Walter N. Tobriner (chairman), D.C. Board of
Commissioners
Brig. Gen. Robert E. Mathe, U.S. Army Corps of
Engineers, D.C. Board of Commissioners
Schuyler Lowe of the D.C. Department of General
Administration
Lt. Col. Tom H. Reynolds, U.S. Army Corps of
Engineers, D.C. assistant engineering commissioner

Representing Maryland:
James P. Gleason (first vice chairman), representing
Montgomery County and the Washington Suburban
Transit Commission
Carlton R. Sickles, chairman of Washington Suburban
Transit Commission, representing Prince George's
County
Rose C. Kramer, secretary of the Montgomery County
Council, representing Washington Suburban Transit
Commission
John H. Marburger, Prince George's County administra-
tor of public works, representing Washington
Suburban Transit Commission

Representing Virginia:
Frederick A. Babson (second vice chairman), Fairfax
County supervisor, representing Northern Virginia
Transportation Commission
Harold J. Casto, chairman of the Arlington County
Board of Supervisors, representing Northern Virginia
Transportation Commission
Lee M. Rhoads, vice mayor of the City of Falls Church,
representing Northern Virginia Transportation
Commission
Nicholas A. Colasanto, vice mayor of the City of
Alexandria, representing Northern Virginia
Transportation Commission

Metro's first Board of Directors—February 20, 1967.
Front row, from left: Sickles, Casto, Gleason, Tobriner, Babson, Mathe.
Back row: Marburger, Kramer, Lowe, Rhoads, Reynolds

Gen. Jackson Graham was a native of Portland, Ore. where he had worked for his father's Pacific Bridge Company, one of the contractors chosen to build Boulder Dam on the Colorado River. He was a 1936 graduate of the University of Oregon where he had served as student body president. He was a battalion and regiment commander during World War II in Europe and later in Korea. From 1963 to 1966 he served as Director of Civil Works for the Corps of Engineers overseeing a $25 billion program to develop water resources. He retired from the Army in 1967 at 52, whereupon he accepted the job of Metro's general manager and was appointed on March 17, 1967.

The new agency coexisted with NCTA for seven months. The NCTA expired on October 1, 1967, and all of its 29 staff members were transferred to WMATA.

One of the first orders of business for the new Metro Board was to hire a general manager. Administrator Mc-

Carter elected to serve as a senior consultant. For the general manager, the new Board of Directors chose a man with impeccable credentials: Maj. Gen. Jackson Graham of the U.S. Army Corps of Engineers. Warren Quenstedt was appointed deputy general manager.

Gen. Graham had many personal acquaintances in Congress who respected his ability and integrity. He immediately began familiarizing himself with the issues involved in building a new rail transit system. He visited San Francisco's new Bay Area Rapid Transit district (BART) to learn from its experiences.

1974
July 24 Metro installs its first bus passenger shelter. By 1986, 828 shelters are in place.
September 1 Metrobus places last of 620 buses ordered from AM General into service.

November 26 President Ford signs amendment to 1974 Urban Mass Transportation Act providing first operating subsidies for transit from Highway Trust Fund.

1975
July 10 Metro Board simplifies Metrobus fare structure in suburban areas effective September 1.

July 24 Metro Board approves addition of Shady Grove station and 2.7 miles of line to Rockville route subject to federal and local funding. Later, when Franconia and Springfield stations are combined, total planned system increases to 99.8 miles.

The Metro Board of Directors approves the Adopted Regional System, March 1, 1968. *Front row, from left:* Jay E. Ricks, Thomas W. Fletcher, Walter E. Fauntroy, James P. Gleason, Frederick A. Babson and Carlton R. Sickles. *Back row, from left:* Nicholas A. Colasanto, Polly Shackleton, Joseph Yeldell, Rose C. Kramer, Lee M. Rhoads and Francis J. Aluisi.

Above: A Metro public hearing at Woodson High School, Fairfax County, January 22, 1968.
Below: 1968 map of the "Adopted Regional System" for display at WMATA public hearings.

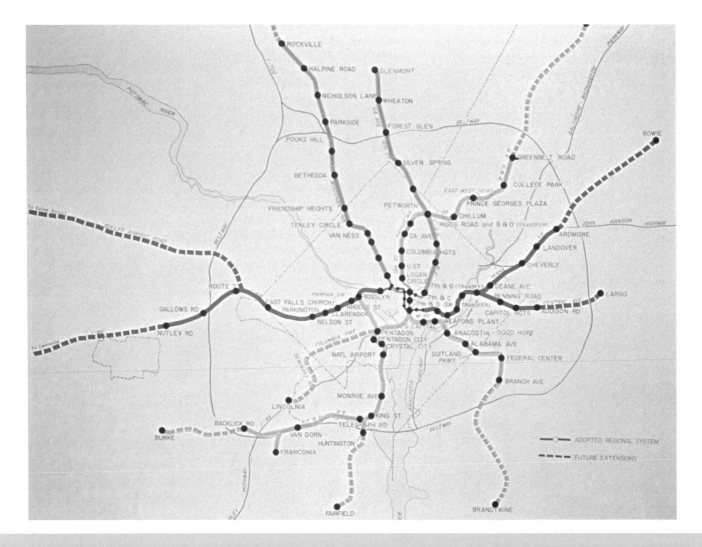

October 10: District of Columbia begins six-year transfer of $2.2 billion of interstate highway funds for Metro construction.

1976
March 27 Six years, three months and 23 days after groundbreaking, Metrorail opens. More than 51,000 people ride free over the 4.2 miles of Metro's Phase 1. Five stations open on Red Line from Rhode Island Ave to Farragut North.

March 29 On first day of revenue service, 19,913 passengers ride on 188 train trips. System is open 6 a.m. to 8 p.m. weekdays and closed on weekends.
June 4 President Ford signs bill authorizing creation of Metro Transit Police.

The Authority then began to refine and solidify plans for the rail system. It held 11 public hearings in January and February of 1968. The WMATA Board approved what they named the "Adopted Regional System" March 1. It resembled the system recommended by NCTA in 1963. It was 97.2 miles in length. At the same time, the Board adopted the name "Metro" for the new transit system.

FUNDING THE SYSTEM

Perhaps the greatest initial challenge to the new agency was to secure the local funding necessary for Metro construction. While a variety of construction funding arrangements have been used over the years, the initial plan relied partially on the sale of bonds. The District of Columbia's share of construction costs would be financed with general District appropriations subject to approval by Congress. In Montgomery County, the County Council imposed a real estate tax to provide its share of Metro's capital construction requirements. In the other six Metro jurisdictions, capital contributions would be raised by the sale of revenue bonds. In the City of Alexandria, the city council had the authority to approve bond sales without submitting them to a popular vote. In Prince George's, Arlington and Fairfax counties, Fairfax City and the City of Falls Church, the bonds would have to be approved in the general election of 1968. It would require serious campaigning to get the bond issues passed. To help accomplish this, the Authority hired John E. Warrington as assistant director of community services.

John E. Warrington had been a news reporter and worked in corporate public relations. He also served as executive secretary to Sen. Styles Bridges of New Hampshire, special assistant to Sen. Kenneth Keating of New York and deputy director of the Federal City Council, a business leadership roundtable group. He served as Metro's connection to the business community.

Mr. Warrington worked closely with a group calling itself "Citizens for Better Regional Transportation." This citizens committee solicited contributions to pay for the bond campaign. The committee was chaired by William Lindholm, president of C&P Telephone Co. It included G. Dewey Arnold of Price Waterhouse; Andrew Parker, president of Woodward and Lothrop department stores; and John Warner of the law firm of Hogan & Hartson.

The campaign got a boost from two sources. On September 8, 1968, WMATA received a full scale engineering mock-up of a Metro rail car. It was first exhibited on the Washington Monument Grounds and then on the south lawn of the White House where it was toured by President Johnson. Following those stops, the car was shown at shopping centers around the area. It generated much excitement among voters considering the bond issue.

Below left: The bond referendum to fund early Metro construction was successful, garnering 70 percent of the votes in November 1968.
Below center: Bond referendum bumper sticker.
Below right: Bond referendum poster.

1977
January 17 Dupont Circle station opens.
January 20 Jimmy Carter's Inaugural Committee charters $170,000 worth of Metrobus service and rents rail system for 2.5 hours to move crowds.

July 1 Blue Line opens from National Airport to Stadium-Armory—18 stations and 12 miles of line. Fare collection switches from exact change fare boxes to automatic fare collection system.

1978
February 6 On snowy day, Red Line begins service to Silver Spring, adding four stations and 5.7 miles of line.

Members of the Metro Board of Directors and spectators unveil the mock-up of the new Metrorail car on the Monument Grounds in September 1968.

Top: Rail car mock-up reflects the color scheme adopted by Metro in 1968.
Bottom: A mock-up of Metro's rail car was displayed on the south lawn of the White House in the fall of 1968. President Johnson greets Metro Board members James Gleason and Frederick Babson along with General Manager Jackson Graham to tour the car.

The other boost came from an unexpected quarter. An economic consulting firm, Development Research Associates, published a study showing that for every $1 invested in Metro construction, $8.80 in benefits would be returned to the community.

The bond issues won in each jurisdiction, garnering the support of about 70 percent of the voters.

April 20 Metro Board approves federally-mandated alternatives analysis. Completed by Metro working with local jurisdictions and the federal government, analysis reconfirms need to finish rail system. Total planned system is now 101 miles.

August 16 Metro, at request of U.S. DOT, presents financial plan for completing and operating Metrorail system to Secretary of Transportation Brock Adams. Adams says, "The federal government agrees with the goal of completing the 100-mile system over the next several years."

September 25 Metrorail extends weekday hours from 8 p.m. to midnight.
September 27, 1978 Metrobus Operator Frank Spadaro wins third annual International Bus Roadeo in Toronto.

ROADBLOCK

The date first proposed for Metro groundbreaking was October 1, 1968. However, in August the D.C. appropriation for fiscal 1969 was passed in Congress without funds for Metro construction. Rep. William H. Natcher of Kentucky, chairman of the D.C. Appropriations SubCommittee, was a strong proponent of the proposed highway system in Washington. He refused to permit the release of Metro funds until the District of Columbia's highway program was underway, including construction of the controversial Three Sisters Bridge. Without the District's share, the bond issues and funds from other jurisdictions would be jeopardized.

Finally, in August 1969 the D.C. City Council relented and approved the Three Sisters Bridge and other highway projects. As a result of citizen protests and later court action, the Three Sisters Bridge was never built.

GROUNDBREAKING

The local capital contributions agreements were signed and in September 1969 the D.C. Appropriations Sub-Committee released the federal share of Metro's construction funds. The legislation passed the full House of Representatives in November and the Senate in December. On December 9, 1969, President Nixon signed the bill authorizing $1.147 billion over the next 10 years. The same day, the Metro Board awarded the first construction contract for $33.7 million. Ground was broken at Judiciary Square that afternoon.

DESIGN AND CONSTRUCTION

In the following years, the Authority continued to struggle with the D.C. Appropriations SubCommittee over the issue of highway versus Metro construction funds. Finally in 1971, with the assistance of the Nixon administration, the full House of Representatives reversed the decision of its Appropriations Committee and released all of the funds for fiscal 1971 and 1972.

In the meantime, construction was underway. The Lydecker Aqueduct, a 67-year-old underground structure connecting Georgetown and McMillan reservoirs in the

Top: Groundbreaking at Judiciary Square, December 9, 1969.
Bottom: Judiciary Square groundbreaking, December 9, 1969. Seven dignitaries turned the ceremonial first shovel of dirt to start 31 years of construction on Metro's 103-mile Adopted Regional System. *From left:* Walter E. Washington, mayor of the District of Columbia; John A. Volpe, U.S. Secretary of Transportation; Frederick A. Babson, chairman of the WMATA Board of Directors; Gilbert Hahn, chairman of the D.C. City Council; Gladys Noon Spellman, chairman of the Washington Suburban Transit Commission. (Maryland Governor Marvin Mandel and Northern Virginia Transportation Commission Chairman Lee M. Rhoads are obscured behind Mr. Babson and Mr. Hahn.)

September 30 Metrorail begins Saturday service 8 a.m. to midnight. Service also includes three federal holidays in addition to July 4—Columbus Day, Veterans Day and Washington's Birthday.

November 20 Orange Line opening to New Carrollton begins Metrorail service to Prince George's County. Segment includes Deanwood and Minnesota Ave. stations in District of Columbia and Cheverly, Landover and New Carrollton in Prince George's County.

1979
February 19 Blizzard on Washington's Birthday causes three-day shutdown of Metrorail. Metrobuses unable to move on first day but provide partial service on second and third days. Full service, rail and bus, restored on fourth day.

Metro's Operations Control Center building opens in the spring of 1974.

Top: Some historic structures had to be relocated to make room for Metro. Here the historic Adas Israel synagogue is moved from the site of the future Metro headquarters building at 6th & G streets NW to its new home at 3rd and G in 1969. Adas Israel was the first synagogue in Washington, and WMATA donated the building to the Jewish Historical Society.
Center: General Manager Jackson Graham and Roy Dodge, Metro's first director of construction.
Bottom: Rohr car bodies are manufactured in Winder, Ga. in the early 1970s.

District of Columbia, was reinforced. The Metro Red Line would pass over the aqueduct as it crossed Rock Creek on its way out Connecticut Avenue NW.

At the same time, design concepts were developed. Metro would be a standard gauge, conventional steel wheel on steel rail system with two main tracks serving each line.

Even though an engineering prototype of the proposed transit car had been previewed, a final design was needed. That job fell to Louis T. Klauder and Associates (LTK) working with Sundberg-Ferar, Inc. of Southfield, Mich.

Metro selected Rohr Industries, an aerospace firm based in Chula Vista, Calif., to build the first 300 cars, which it produced at its plant in Winder, Ga. Rohr had built the cars for San Francisco's BART system, which opened in 1972.

Metro is among the biggest and longest lasting single public works projects ever undertaken in the United States. Bechtel Corp. was chosen to oversee construction. One of their greatest challenges took place before actual tunnel digging could begin. The foundations of several buildings in the city, including some historic structures, had to be reinforced before tunneling could be done near or beneath them. Notable among these was the National Portrait Gallery in the historic U.S. Patent Office at 8th and F streets NW, directly above the proposed Gallery Place station on the Red Line. Reinforcing this structure with 430 70-foot-deep pilings took contractors four years.

In addition to constructing tunnels, Metro built a new headquarters at 5th and F streets NW to house its staff and technologically advanced Operations Control Center. It was first occupied in the spring of 1974. In 1985 it was dedicated to the memory of Metro's first general manager and is now called the Jackson Graham Building.

April 2 Metrobus tests wheelchair lift-equipped buses on seven routes.
June 17 Forty-three articulated (bend-in-the-middle) buses begin Metrobus service on Benning Road line in District of Columbia.

July 1 Metrobus begins regular route wheelchair lift-equipped service on 12 lines.
July 12 Metro announces award of $75.3 million contract to Italian firm of Breda Costruzioni Ferroviarie for 94 rail cars with option for additional 200.

September 2 Metrorail begins Sunday service from 10 a.m. to 6 p.m.

INCREASING COSTS AND
NEW RESPONSIBILITIES

In the early 1970s, forces and events converged to permanently change Metro. Inflation caused the area's financially strapped private bus companies to threaten to stop running for good. In 1972 Congress took up the issue with the belief that a unified bus and rail system would benefit the region. In October, President Nixon signed a bill authorizing WMATA to buy the four failing companies and operate their service under its own auspices. In early 1973, WMATA made the purchases. Essentially overnight, Metro's staff jumped from 350 to about 3,500.

The Authority immediately began to modernize the newly named Metrobus system. Public acquisition gave the Authority 1,744 vehicles in various states of repair. Metro ordered 620 new buses and scheduled some older buses for renovation. All acquired vehicles were repainted with the new Metrobus colors. Bus shelters were installed at several locations and new bus stop signs were installed throughout the system. Metrobus was operating sooner than many people thought it would be.

The same inflation that forced the public takeover of the private bus companies was impacting Metro system construction. From 1969 to 1974 construction wage rates more than doubled. Construction materials costs also rose rapidly. Eventually Metro was forced to revise its estimate to complete the 98-mile system from $2.5 billion to $4.5 billion. Where the extra money would come from was anybody's guess.

The answer came in 1973 with the passage of the Federal Aid Highway Act which established a new provision for use of monies in the Highway Trust Fund. The act gave each state the option of deciding not to build some part of its interstate highways and using the funds, instead, for transit projects. At first the District of Columbia was exempt from that provision but eventually the District's share of the Highway Trust Fund also became eligible. Soon, the District began a six-year transfer of $2 billion to Metro as it eliminated several unwanted highway projects. At about the same time, Virginia transferred $100 million to Metro. Maryland transferred $36 million.

During these difficult years Metro's funding quest received the support of the Ford administration. U.S. Secretary of Transportation William Coleman took the unusual step of guaranteeing Metro's funding for the complete system until

Metro acquires old DC Transit buses as part of the 1973 bus company acquisition.

AM General buses—the first ones to be ordered after the acquisition of the private bus companies—arrive at Metro's Bladensburg garage.

The K Street Freeway: Red Line customers may have noticed that the vaulted arch of the Farragut North station does not extend the complete length of the platform. At the outbound end, where the Connecticut Connection is located, the ceiling drops to a low flat box. That dropped ceiling was built to accommodate an element of the proposed K Street Freeway, one of the many highway projects that were cancelled once it became permissible to transfer Highway Trust Fund monies to transit projects. It remains as a potent reminder of what might have been.

December 1 Orange Line begins service to Ballston station. Four stations—Court House, Clarendon, Virginia Sq-GMU and Ballston—and 2.63 miles are added to system.

1980
January 3 President Carter signs Stark-Harris bill authorizing $1.7 billion in federal funds to finish Metrorail construction.
November 22 Benning Road, Capitol Heights and Addison Road stations open, adding 3.5 miles to Blue Line.

1981
June 25 Metro orders additional 200 rail cars from Breda Costruzioni Ferroviarie for about $200 million.

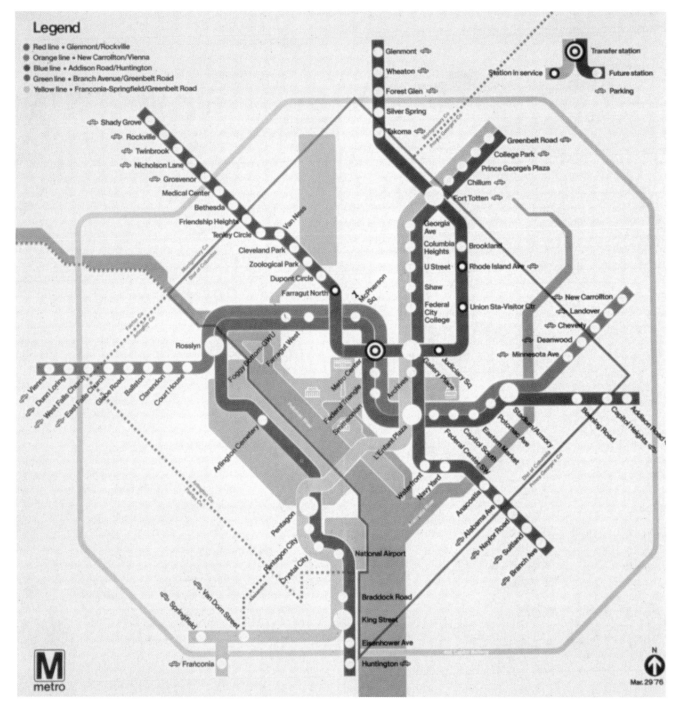

Legend

- ● Red line • Glenmont/Rockville
- ● Orange line • New Carrollton/Vienna
- ● Blue line • Addison Road/Huntington
- ● Green line • Branch Avenue/Greenbelt Road
- ○ Yellow line • Franconia-Springfield/Greenbelt Road

⊙ Transfer station
○ Station in service
■ Future station
⇔ Parking

M metro

Mar. 29 '76

Congress could be persuaded to release Washington's share of the Highway Trust Fund. That way Metro construction could continue while the funding issue was debated.

On Saturday, March 27, 1976, the first segment of the Metro system began operating with free rides between Rhode Island Avenue and Farragut North on the Red Line. The first day of revenue service was Monday, March 29. Between then and now more than 98 additional miles have been built and placed into service. The final price of the full 103-mile system is $9.4 billion, of which $6.4 billion was contributed by direct federal appropriation and $3 billion was paid by the local governments. Its replacement value is estimated to be $21 billion. The rapid transit system now costs more than $750 million a year to operate and maintain and Metro has embarked on a massive program to renovate the oldest parts of the system. Metrorail and Metrobus together now carry more than one million passengers every weekday.

November 12 Metro Board decides to rebuild more than 600 Metrobuses. Metrobus carries its one-billionth passenger.

December 5 Van Ness-UDC, Cleveland Park and Woodley Park-Zoo stations open, adding 2.07 miles to Red Line.

1982
January 13 First Metrorail passenger fatalities occur when a Metro train derails at a crossover switch between Federal Triangle and Smithsonian. Metro's accident occurs in the midst of a major snowstorm and is preceded by the crash of an airliner into 14th Street Bridge and the Potomac River.

October 11 Metro dedicates Montgomery Division, its first new Metrobus garage since 1973 bus acquisition.

Opposite page: Metrorail's first system map.
Right: Children enjoy opening day festivities at Rhode Island Avenue station, March 27, 1976.
Below: Jackson Graham (center) with D.C. Mayor Walter Washington and Fairfax County Supervisor Joe Alexander, both members of the Metro Board of Directors, February 27, 1976, one month before opening day.

Jackson Graham retired from Metro in January 1976, just two months before the first trains began to roll. His legacy is nothing less than "America's Subway." According to Cleatus Barnett, Metro's longest-serving Board member, "General Graham succeeded where any other would have failed. His skills, talent and drive brought Metro into being and put it on a road so nothing could stop it."

Gen. Graham's influence is still felt in the Metro organization. "Manage by example," he said in 1974. "Be firm, fair and human. Avoid bombast and rhetoric. Follow modest habits. Encourage cooperation and good feeling between offices and individuals. Step on bureaucratic jealousies. Set standards for all activity from paperwork to construction, and require correction often enough to sustain them."

1983
April 30 Yellow Line begins operating from Gallery Pl-Chinatown to National Airport, crossing Potomac on Metro's Charles R. Fenwick Bridge. Segment includes new station, Archives-Navy Mem'l, and opens second platform level at both Gallery Pl-Chinatown and L'Enfant Plaza transfer stations.

May First of new Breda Metrorail cars arrive.
October 30 Amtrak opens its New Carrollton rail station with direct interface with Metro's New Carrollton station.

December 17 Yellow Line opens from National Airport to Huntington, adding Braddock Road, King Street, Eisenhower Avenue and Huntington stations and 4.3 miles to rail system. Huntington is first station in Fairfax County.

Metro, the long awaited rapid transit system for the Nation's Capital, began revenue operations March 29, 1976, on its first 4.6 miles of line amidst cheers of approval from its first riders.

"It's time to stop talking and start riding," said WMATA Board Chairman Sterling Tucker as he and other dignitaries cut a ribbon at the opening ceremonies on the morning of Saturday, March 27.

Washingtonians flocked to their new system in numbers that surprised even the most optimistic Metro officials. Metro carried 51,260 free riders on opening day. The estimate was 10,000.

During the first several weeks of operation, passenger counts were three times the estimates—about 25,000 a day. A new rush hour—mid-day—emerged. At the end of the fifth week, more than 600,000 passengers had ridden the system and some $247,395 in fares were collected. The success of the first few weeks and the third rush hour a day attracted national attention.

Cheers were commonplace during the first week as the Metro trains entered stations with crowded platforms and mezzanines. The excitement of the new system elicited applause for even the most routine operations. A train operator who stopped the train and explained on the intercom that he was being replaced by an operator on the next shift got a round of applause.

Lunchers, shoppers, sightseers and joy-riders descended into the downtown stations to ride standing-room-only to restaurants, specialty shops, department stores or just to examine Metro from the inside. The transit authority adjusted its regular 10-minute, mid-day schedule to accommodate the noontime crowds.

Although the Metro opening segment is relatively short in relation to the projected 100-mile system*, it provides a valuable link between Northeast and Northwest Washington. In the Northeast, Metro connects with two major collection points for inbound and outbound commuters, the Rhode Island Avenue corridor for bus and car commuters from Prince George's County, Md. and the surrounding District of Columbia neighborhood and Union Station for railroad commuters. In the Northwest, the system provides easy access to both the F and G Street shopping and business districts, and the Connecticut Avenue commercial area. Mid-point on the run is Judiciary Square station, which serves the federal courts area.

Ribbon-cutting ceremony at Rhode Island Ave station, March 27, 1976. *Front row cutting the ribbon,from left:* Bill Fauntroy, Metro staff member (holding the far end of the ribbon); Walter J. McCarter, former administrator of NCTA; C. Darwin Stolzenbach, former administrator of NCTA; Metro Board members Norman L. Christeller (Maryland), Rev. Jerry A. Moore Jr. (District of Columbia), Carlton R. Sickles (Maryland), John P. Shacochis (Virginia) and Francis W. White (Maryland); Marvin Mandel, governor of Maryland; Metro Board member James E. Coates (District of Columbia); Rep. Herbert Harris II (D-Va.) and former Metro Board member; Theodore C. Lutz, deputy secretary of U.S. Department of Transportation and future Metro general manager; Robert Patricelli, administrator of the U.S. Urban Mass Transportation Administration; Metro Board members Joseph Alexander (Virginia) and, at the podium, Sterling Tucker (District of Columbia), Board chairman; Walter E. Washington, mayor of the District of Columbia and Metro Board member, is obscured behind Mr. Tucker. Immediately to the right of the podium: Cody Pfanstiehl, Metro director of community services; Jackson Graham, retired Metro general manager; Warren D. Quenstedt, then acting Metro general manager.

Transit authority officials, years in advance of the Phase I opening, referred to it as the "debugging phase." They knew that unforeseeable problems, they hoped minor ones, would surface when real passengers were riding the trains on a regular schedule. A few bugs did appear during the first week of operations. On opening day, crush loads of passengers caused doors to bind, stalling trains in the stations. There were also some motor overload and brake problems.

As operating experience accumulated, the delays became shorter.

Opening day crowds of 4,000 persons waited at the entrances to Rhode Island Avenue and Farragut North stations most of the day. The crowd at Farragut North stretched for blocks extending the full length of DeSales Street (next to the Mayflower Hotel) as people waited, mostly in good humor, to ride the trains free. At Rhode Island Avenue, two lines, three to five persons across, extended several hundred yards each. Traffic on Rhode Island Avenue and Connecticut Avenue was stalled for several blocks at times because of the long lines.

Opening day anecdotes abounded as Washingtonians reacted in a carnival-like mood to their new train system. "I've been working on the railroad," sang one early passenger as other persons on the packed car chimed in. A news correspondent from Moscow, impressed by his first ride, told a Metro employee that Metro was a really fine system. He claimed a certain expertise on the subject since, he observed, "Moscow has the best subway in the world." A young man in red beard rushed to a man wearing a Metro badge aboard a train and pumped his hand emphatically while repeating, "amazing, absolutely amazing. I would never believe it."

On the Sunday following opening, congregations of several downtown churches gathered in the spacious Metro Center station following their regular services and performed a liturgy of celebration, thanksgiving, and dedication to the new Metro. The celebration included a processional down the escalator of the station with the New York Avenue Presbyterian Church choir singing Faith of Our Fathers and Stand Up, Stand Up for Jesus.

From the small 4.6-mile, Phase I line, the Metro operation will grow year by year, to a 100 mile, 87 station regional system* serving Washington, D.C. and the Maryland and Virginia suburbs of the capital city.

Already, more than half of the system is under construction or completed. Cost of the system is estimated at upwards of $4.676 billion. The return to the region in the long run, will be $3 for each $1 invested, according to an independent cost survey conducted in 1968.

Metro is the largest rapid rail transit system ever built under one plan at one time. This single project approach, according to its planners, will save millions of dollars compared to the many-project approach extending over many years.

Opening day crowds wait in line for free rides at Rhode Island Ave station, March 27, 1976.

On opening day, Saturday, March 27, 1976, people line up for free rides at Rhode Island Ave station.

Rhode Island Ave station, March 2000, 24 years after opening day.

Article published in the "Metro Memo" newsletter in May 1976 *At that time the Adopted Regional System was 100 miles in length with 87 stations.

President Carter signs the Stark-Harris bill into law, January 3, 1980. *Front row from left:* Joseph Alexander, Metro Board member (Virginia); Martha Pennino, Fairfax County supervisor; Rep. Gladys Noon Spellman (Maryland), former Metro Board member; Sen. Paul Sarbanes (Maryland); Rep. Herbert Harris II (Virginia), former Metro Board member and co-sponsor of the Stark-Harris bill; Rep. Joseph L. Fisher (Virginia), former Metro Board member. *Others pictured:* John P. Shacochis, Fairfax County supervisor and former Metro Board member (to the right behind Rep. Spellman); Between Sen. Sarbanes and Rep. Harris, from left: U.S. Secretary of Transportation Neil Goldschmitt; Cleatus E. Barnett, Metro Board member (Maryland); Rev. Jerry A. Moore Jr., Metro Board member (District of Columbia); Sen. Charles "Mac" Mathias (Maryland). *Official White House photo*

Dignitaries sing happy birthday to Metro at the 10th anniversary celebration March 29, 1986 in the Old Post Office Pavillion. *From left:* Rev. Walter E. Fauntroy, Metro Board member Carlton R. Sickles (Maryland), UMTA Administrator Ralph Stanley, Metro General Manager Carmen E. Turner, Metro Board member Frank Smith Jr. (District of Columbia), Virginia Secretary of Transportation Vivian Watts, District of Columbia Mayor Marion Barry, Virginia state Sen. Edward M. Holland (Arlington), Metro Board member Robert B. Ostrom (Maryland).

ALTERNATIVES ANALYSIS

The first rail segment had been operating only a few months when the federal government required that the region seriously consider cutting the Adopted Regional System by about half. In 1976 the administrator of the Urban Mass Transportation Administration, Robert Patricelli, reasoned that circumstances had changed since 1968. Less expensive transit options might be substituted for the planned rail system.

Patricelli called for an alternatives analysis to be conducted by WMATA, the U.S. Department of Transportation and the Metropolitan Washington Council of Governments. For nearly two years, Metro awarded no construction contracts while the analysis was being done.

When it was finished in May 1978, the analysis confirmed the need to build the ARS. It recommended shifting the Branch Avenue route to end at Rosecroft Raceway, deleting the Springfield station in favor of the Franconia-Springfield station, adopting the S-curve alignment on the Greenbelt segment and substituting West Hyattsville station for the Chillum station. The rest of the system remained essentially unchanged. The ARS would now be 101 miles in length.

On August 16, 1978, WMATA presented the analysis and a financial plan for completing and operating the ARS to Secretary of Transportation Brock Adams who received it favorably. The Board's decision favoring the Rosecroft alignment was challenged in court, however, and the issue was not settled until March 1984. The Board adopted the current alignment and, in December 1984, changed the terminus back to Branch Avenue. That increased the system to 103 miles. The Rosecroft decision and the litigation that followed delayed the Anacostia segment by more than five years and the remaining segment to Branch Avenue by more than a decade. It took no less of a figure than Carmen Turner to assume the role of general manager and break the impasse to get things moving again.

INFLATION

Double-digit inflation in the late 1970s combined with delays beyond Metro's control again drove the projected cost of finishing the system beyond earlier estimates. Congress passed the Stark-Harris bill in late 1979 authorizing $1.7 billion to finish building the system. President Carter signed the bill on January 3, 1980. Over the next four years, the region

1984
August 25 Red Line begins operating 6.81-mile segment to Grosvenor including Tenleytown-AU, Friendship Heights, Bethesda and Medical Center stations.

September 13 Metro Board adopts plan to complete 89.5 miles of 101-mile system using Stark-Harris federal funding and local matching grants.
December 13: Metro Board selects Branch Ave terminus and St. Elizabeths alignment for southern portion of Green Line, increasing system mileage to 103.

December 15 Red Line opens 6.98-mile extension, including four stations—White Flint, Twinbrook, Rockville and Shady Grove.

1985
April 11 Board approves 2.5-mile alignment of Green Line between Columbia Heights and Fort Totten stations in District of Columbia.

worked closely with Urban Mass Transportation Administration to meet new requirements for receiving the authorized funds. All the while inflation remained at work. By the time Metro met all the requirements, September 13, 1984, Stark-Harris funds and local matching grants would cover only 89.5 miles. Once again, additional funds were required to finish the system.

At this difficult juncture, a new general manager stepped forward to continue the pioneering ways of her predecessors. Carmen E. Turner broke new ground among transit operations in the United States—she was the first African-American female to serve as general manager of a large urban transit system. She came on the scene just as Metro's future once again looked cloudy.

During the course of her term as Metro's general manager, Mrs. Turner earned a reputation in the transit industry for outstanding leadership. In 1984 Metro faced serious troubles. A court injunction had halted Green Line construction east of Waterfront station, federal construction funds were on hold, the Branch Avenue extension was not funded and procurement of enough rail cars to meet future needs was in doubt. Mrs. Turner set her sights on overcoming these obstacles in spite of the Board's counsel that she probably would be unsuccessful. Over time, her superlative skills in dealing with people generated favor among congressional leaders, and eventually her persistence began to pay off.

Legislation to once again amend the National Capital Transportation Act was introduced in Congress in March 1989, and Mrs. Turner worked closely with the area's congressional delegation to get it passed. It was viewed as a tough sell at a time when the federal government faced difficult budget constraints. Rep. Steny Hoyer spearheaded a very cohesive effort by the area congressional delegation to build support for the legislation from around the country. Despite a veto threat from the administration, the bill passed the House by a comfortable margin of 260-150. On October 27, 1990, Congress gave final approval to re-authorization legislation providing an additional $1.3 billion in federal funding over eight years for construction of the Metro system.

On the heels of these momentous achievements, Mrs. Turner resigned from Metro in December 1990. Her replacement as general manager was David L. Gunn, appointed in March 1991. Along with Carmen Turner, he must be counted among the latter-day transit pioneers in Washington.

Carmen E. Turner (nee Pawley) spent her childhood in Washington, D.C. and graduated from Dunbar High School. She enrolled at Howard University but left college when she married fellow student Frederick B. Turner. When her two sons were in elementary school, she returned to Howard to complete her baccalaureate. Then she went on to earn a master's degree in public administration at American University.

Mrs. Turner joined the civil rights office of the Urban Mass Transportation Administration in 1970. In 1976 she was named acting director of civil rights for U.S. Department of Transportation. She was chosen to be WMATA's first assistant general manager for administration in 1977, and in 1983 she became the first and only general manager chosen from within the organization.

Under Mrs. Turner's leadership Metro was awarded the transit industry's highest honor, the Outstanding Achievement Award from the American Public Transit Association in 1988. The following year, APTA named Mrs. Turner Transit Manager of the Year, and gave her its Jesse L. Haugh Award for the manager "who has done the most to advance the urban transit industry in the United States and Canada."

In December 1990, Mrs. Turner resigned from WMATA to become under secretary of the Smithsonian Institution. This made her the second ranking official of the world's largest museum and research complex and its chief operating officer.

Mrs. Turner died on April 9, 1992, at the age of 61. On October 20, 1992, she was inducted into APTA's Transit Hall of Fame, the first woman to be so honored. In May 1995 WMATA dedicated the Smithsonian Metrorail station in her honor.

July 17 Metro modifies safety plan to include passenger-activated escape doors in the event of a fire aboard train.
December 9 Metro sales facility opens at Metro Center station.

1986
June 7 Orange Line grows by 9.11 miles with opening of East Falls Church, West Falls Church, Dunn Loring and Vienna stations in Fairfax County.

July 16 Metro and Urban Mass Transportation Administration sign full-funding agreement releasing fiscal 1985 and 1986 capital funds needed to continue building 89.5-mile system funded under Stark-Harris authorization.

October 7 Metro receives APTA Management Innovation Award for its Construction Safety Awareness Program.

David L. Gunn is a native of Boston. He earned his B.A. from Harvard College and his MBA from the Harvard Graduate School of Business. He managed three of the nation's major transit properties in addition to Metro. He served as director of operations at the Massachusetts Bay Transportation Authority in Boston, general manager and chief operations officer of the Southeastern Pennsylvania Transportation Authority in Philadelphia, president of the New York City Transit Authority and general manager of the Toronto Transit Commission. He was Metro's general manager from March 1991 to March 1994.

Richard A. White became the seventh general manager of Metro on August 12, 1996. Before that, he served as deputy general manager and then general manager of the Bay Area Rapid Transit District in Oakland, Calif. He also worked in management positions at New Jersey Transit Corp. and U.S. DOT Urban Mass Transit Administration.

A native of Andover, Mass., he holds a bachelor of arts in political science from the University of Massachusetts and a master's degree in public administration from the Maxwell School of Citizenship and Public Affairs at Syracuse University.

David Gunn's most enduring contribution was the creation of Fast Track, a concept that enabled the remaining Metro construction projects to be completed before inflation could again erode Metro's funding. One of the innovative features of Fast Track was the decision to borrow construction funds from commercial lending institutions which would be repaid when future federal and local contributions were received. That way construction remained on track.

When funding was stretched, competition arose among the political jurisdictions represented on the Metro Board to see whose project would be funded next. Mr. Gunn's solution was to do it all simultaneously. He and Deputy General Manager George Miller developed a financial plan that permitted the Franconia-Springfield, Glenmont and Branch Avenue segments to move ahead simultaneously.

On December 19, 1991, the Metro Board approved the scheduling and funding for Fast Track. That schedule called for completion of the last 13.5 miles of the rail system using the funds in the 1990 federal authorization. Clearing this final hurdle enabled WMATA to award all remaining Metro construction contracts and assured the completion of the 103-mile system. The additional cost savings have been applied toward the purchase of new rail cars and the completion of the Branch Avenue Yard.

REGIONAL MOBILITY: RENEWED COMMITMENT TO THE METROBUS SYSTEM

Richard A. White was sworn in as Metro's seventh general manager in August 1996. At that time WMATA and its constituent local governments began to reconsider the role of Metrobus in the region's overall transportation system. The trend in the preceding decade had been to move away from Metrobus in favor of locally operated bus services.

Later that year, Congress mandated that the parties reach a consensus on ways to revitalize bus service in the Washington area. In response, a Regional Mobility Panel was established. The Panel adopted a plan on September 26, 1997, specifying that Metrobus service would be preserved and promoted as an essential element of the region's transportation infrastructure.

The Metro Board of Directors approved the plan on October 9, 1997. The plan said, in effect, that thereafter the regional Metrobus system would be planned, funded and operated in a manner similar to the Metrorail system. Before the plan, all Metrobus services were offered at the discretion of the local governments. The plan gives WMATA decision-making autonomy, under an approved funding formula, over routes that are recognized for their regional significance—about 75 percent of all Metrobus service. The remaining 25 percent of Metrobus routes are designated non-regional services that remain under local control.

October 18 For second year in a row, Metro mechanics from Southeastern Division win International Bus Maintenance Roadeo. MTA in Baltimore is host.

1987
January 22 and 25 Two major storms dump total of 25 inches of snow on region, shutting down everything including Metrorail surface operations. Within next two months, Metro undertakes major winterization program to improve performance of rail and bus during extreme snow and ice conditions. Bulk of program is complete by year's end.

June 19 At 4:27 a.m. on a Friday, 21 CSXT freight cars derail into Metro's right-of-way north of Takoma station. Metrorail is not operating at this hour. Although no injuries result, Metro suffers demolished track, ties, ballast, fencing, automatic train control equipment and communications lines. Extraordinary Metro repair efforts restore service by Monday morning, June 22.

FARE RESTRUCTURING

In keeping with the objectives of the Regional Mobility process, Metro dramatically restructured Metrobus fares in June 1999. This initiative replaced a complex system of zone fares, interstate crossing charges and transfer charges with the concept of simplicity and value. Most Metrobus fares are now a flat $1.10. Bus-to-bus transfers are free and a new regional discount policy allows customers to transfer between Metrorail and any other bus system in the region.

This fare restructuring has resulted in dramatic ridership growth. Between 1997 and 2000, Metrorail ridership increased 19 percent, to a weekday average of 586,000 daily trips in the last half of 2000. In that same time period Metrobus ridership rose 22 percent, to a weekday average of 500,000 daily trips. That brings total ridership to more than one million daily passenger trips systemwide, a 20 percent increase. Metrorail is now the second busiest rail rapid transit operation in the United States after New York City.

CLOSING OF THE LATEST CHAPTER IN METRO'S HISTORY

In 1890 the U.S. Bureau of the Census announced the disappearance of a contiguous frontier line in the western United States. Historian Frederick Jackson Turner said, "...the frontier has gone, and with its going has closed the first period of American history."

One might argue that Richard White is the final transit pioneer, presiding over the closing of the rail rapid transit frontier in Washington. With the opening of the final segment of the Green Line to Branch Avenue on January 13, 2001, Metrorail's Adopted Regional System—a version of which was originally approved 33 years ago—was completed. However, other challenges are on Metro's horizon. By improving core capacity, renewing and replacing Metro's aging infrastructure and extending the system to serve Washington's rapidly developing suburbs, Metro will continue to play a vital role in the economic health of the National Capital Area. The dawn of the 21st century coincides with the beginning of a new era for Metro as the region's transportation leader.

Metro General Manager Richard A. White presents a commemorative poster to Maryland Governor Parris Glendening at the opening ceremony at Branch Avenue, January 13, 2001, celebrating the completion of the 103-mile Adopted Regional System

Metro's current Board of Directors—January 2001.
Standing left to right: Carlton R. Sickles, Maryland; David A. Catania, District of Columbia; John P. Davey, Maryland; Calvin T. Nophlin, District of Columbia; William D. Euille, Virginia; Dana Kauffman, Virginia
Seated left to right: Cleatus E. Barnett, Maryland; Jim Graham, District of Columbia; Decatur W. Trotter, Maryland; Gladys W. Mack, District of Columbia; Christopher Zimmerman, Virginia; Katherine K. Hanley, Virginia

September 5 It happens again, only this time 14 derailing CSXT cars tear up Metrorail right-of-way between Takoma and Fort Totten stations at 11:23 p.m. Metro restores service Wednesday afternoon, September 9. Incident leads to intensive safety precautions and studies by Metro and CSXT.

1988
January 8 A 10-inch snowfall challenges transit system which is operating under full emergency snow plan mobilization. Buses and trains run without major problems.

February 3 Metrorail sets ridership record of 564,265 trips on day Washingtonians welcome Redskins home from Super Bowl victory with parade.

March 17 CSXT and Metro announce joint recommendations to improve safety along shared rail corridors.
April 28 For fifth consecutive year, Metro Board adopts budget with no fare increase.

William H. (Pop) Saunders, a track laborer during the early part of his 29-year career in Washington transit, was one of the first to master the operation of the sleek Metro trains. Saunders was among the first six Metrobus operators selected for train operations during the start-up testing program.

In 1946, following service in the South Pacific in World War II, he joined the Capital Transit Company as a laborer, the only job open to him. "I was called a Laborer D," he said, "which means we did everything." "Everything" included repairing and replacing trolley rail along the old Glen Echo, Cabin John and Benning Road lines.

For the nearly 10 years that racial discrimination kept him from becoming a motorman, Saunders was assigned various jobs in the ways and structures division of the transit company. This included maintenance work on transit buildings and work on the electrical trucks used to maintain the lines. It also included a job with an unappealing title—pit man.

The pit man, Saunders explained, stood in a pit beneath the tracks to switch the electrical traction current from underground cables to overhead wires. Overhead cable was not permitted in the downtown area of the city, so streetcars had to switch from an overhead to an underground power source at a location on each line known as the "plow pit."

At last, the opportunity to become a streetcar motorman opened to Saunders. "Charlie Miller, my foreman, told us they were going to hire some blacks," said Saunders, recalling that Capital Transit had been under pressure to do so. This, he said, was in 1955.

Saunders was the first to apply. However, the ways and structures division had a backlog of work because of a labor strike, and Saunders stayed on his old job a while longer to help out. He recalled that there were four or five other black motormen at Capital Transit by the time he actually started operating streetcars.

"I fell in love with streetcars," he said, and apparently his ardor never cooled in spite of his long experience driving buses following the demise of Washington's streetcars.

Saunders became the senior member of that group of six pioneer train operators for the Metro system. Mr. Saunders' son, Ron, now manages the collection of Metro's traffic data used to plan service.

GROWING A RAIL SYSTEM BRANCH BY BRANCH

Even though it was conceived as a unified system, Metrorail has been built in segments. The original 103-mile system now complete, Metro serves 83 stations. Here are the opening dates of each completed segment:

March 29, 1976 First segment opens with 4.5 miles with five stations: Rhode Island Ave, Union Station, Judiciary Sq, Metro Center, Farragut North.

Dec. 15, 1976 Gallery Pl-Chinatown opens following a waiver of the administrator of the General Services Administration requiring the elevator to be working by July 1, 1977.

Jan. 17, 1977 Dupont Circle station opens, adding one-third of a mile to the system.

July 1, 1977 Blue Line opens between National Airport and Stadium-Armory stations, adding 17 stations and 12 miles of line. Metro Center lower level begins operation.

Feb. 6, 1978 Red Line begins service to Silver Spring, adding four stations and 5.7 miles of line.

Opening day festivities at Silver Spring station. Metro Board member Cleatus E. Barnett speaks from the podium. To the right are Board member Joseph Wholey of Virginia, Metro General Manager Theodore C. Lutz, and UMTA Administrator Richard S. Page, who would be appointed Metro general manager 16 months later.

Nov. 20, 1978 Orange Line extends from Stadium-Armory to New Carrollton, adding 7.4 miles and five stations.

Dec. 1, 1979 Orange Line extension from Rosslyn to Ballston-MU adds four stations and 2.63 miles of line.

Nov. 22, 1980 Blue Line extends from Stadium-Armory to Addison Road-Seat Pleasant adding three stations and 3.6 miles of line.

Dec. 5, 1980 Red Line extends from Dupont Circle to Van Ness-UDC, adding 2.1 miles and three stations.

April 30, 1983 Yellow Line opens from Gallery Pl-Chinatown to National Airport, crossing the Potomac on Metro's Charles R. Fenwick bridge. Segment includes one new station, Archives-Navy Mem'l, and opens the lower level platform at Gallery Pl-Chinatown and the upper level platform at L'Enfant Plaza.

Dec. 17, 1983 Yellow Line opens 4.3 mile segment from National Airport to Huntington, the first station in Fairfax County.

Aug. 25, 1984 Red Line opens 6.8-mile segment to Grosvenor-Strathmore, adding five stations.

Dec. 15, 1984 Red Line opens seven-mile segment to Shady Grove adding four more stations.

June 7, 1986 Orange Line is completed with the opening of nine miles and four stations between Ballston-MU and Vienna/Fairfax-GMU.

Sept. 22, 1990 Red Line opens a 3.2-mile, two station segment from Silver Spring to Wheaton.

May 11, 1991 First three Green Line stations open between Gallery Pl-Chinatown and U St/African-Amer Civil War Memorial/Cardozo. Yellow Line is completed with its extension to Mt Vernon Sq/7th St-Convention Center.

June 15, 1991 Blue Line extends 3.7 miles from King Street to Van Dorn Street in Alexandria.

Dec. 28, 1991 Green Line opens 2.9-mile segment from L'Enfant Plaza to Anacostia, adding three stations.

Dec. 11, 1993 Green Line opens eight-mile segment between Fort Totten and Greenbelt, adding four stations.

June 28, 1997 Blue Line extends 3.4 miles from Van Dorn Street to Franconia-Springfield. Blue Line is now complete. The Franconia-Springfield station is a major hub for Metrobus and local transit bus services, commuter bus, Virginia Railway Express commuter rail service and Metrorail. It is named the Joe Alexander Transit Center in honor of Virginia's longest-serving member of Metro's Board of Directors, pictured above.

July 25, 1998 Red Line is completed with the one-station, 1.4-mile extension from Wheaton to Glenmont.

Sept. 18, 1999 Mid-city segment of the Green Line opens, connecting Fort Totten and U St/African-Amer Civil War Memorial/Cardozo.

Jan. 13, 2001 Extension of the Green Line from Anacostia to Branch Avenue adds final 6.5 miles of the Adopted Regional System. The Green Line and the 103-mile Adopted Regional System are now complete.

METROBUS OPERATIONS: 1973-2001

When the transit authority began Metrobus operations in 1973, it faced a formidable task: integrating four separate route networks into a unified regional system that was modern and efficient. Immediately after takeover, the Authority applied red, white and blue decals with the new Metrobus logo to the existing fleet. During the first weeks of Metrobus operation, duplicate route numbers were eliminated, new routes were established, boarding and alighting restrictions were dropped during non-rush periods and fares were stabilized.

During the first year of Metrobus operation, the Authority purchased 620 new buses from AM General to guarantee schedules, increase service on existing routes, expand service into areas not previously served and retire older equipment. In April 1974 service was increased on 77 routes, and in July the first of 700 new bus shelters was installed.

In September 1974, changes were made on 136 routes, and a number of express and cross-county routes were inaugurated. New bus lanes were established in October 1974 to speed buses during rush hours.

Progress continued in 1975 and 1976 when the first new Metrobus stop signs were installed and the first of many new Park & Ride lots were opened. A new systemwide fare structure went into effect, creating uniformly-sized zones and consistent fares throughout the Metro service area.

In March 1976, with the opening of the Metrorail system, Metro made the first of many route changes to provide convenient connections between the bus and rail systems. With each opening of a segment of Metrorail, the Authority has restructured Metrobus service to complement the rail system.

In 1975, Montgomery County began operating its own Ride On bus service along routes formerly served by Metrobus. Today local bus service is provided by Fairfax County, Fairfax City, the City of Alexandria, Montgomery County and Prince George's County.

Metrobus is always open to new ways to serve its customers. Wheelchair lift-equipped buses are now commonplace. Supplemental holiday service has been available for shoppers during the Christmas season. Express buses from fringe parking lots and new service from downtown to job opportunities in the suburbs serve the changing needs of riders.

A mechanic installs a Metrobus decal on one of the vehicles acquired in the 1973 takeover of the private bus companies.

One of the first Metrobus stop signs installed in 1975.

June 22 Metrobus carries two billionth rider.
August 24 Metrorail carries one-billionth rider.
October 4 American Public Transit Association awards Metro its top honor, the *Public Transportation System Outstanding Achievement Award*. Metro dubbed *America's Subway*.

1989
January 20 Metrorail sets ridership record of 604,000 during inauguration of President Bush.

February 26 Metrobus opens Landover Division bus garage to replace Prince George's Division. Latter becomes Southern Avenue Annex to support service in southern Prince George's County.

November 23 through New Yea Winterization program proves its effectiveness in series of snowfal and record-low temperatures in late fall, early winter. Rail and bus systems operate with minima disruption.

The Metrobus system has served more than 3.2 billion customers since it acquired the private bus companies. Metrobus vehicles have traveled more than 846 million miles—the equivalent of 1,771 round trips to the moon. The result of regional-federal cooperation for more than a quarter-century, Metrobus continues to serve alongside Metrorail as the backbone of the region's public transportation network.

FOOTNOTES TO HISTORY

Georgetown station

It's often asked, "Why is there no Metro station in Georgetown?" Today, in view of the area's traffic jams, a Georgetown Metro station seems like an obvious choice. Popular belief is that the station was originally suggested but was dropped in the face of strong citizen opposition. The reason for its absence is more complex than that.

1. In the 1950s and 1960s, existing residential development and commercial land use patterns in Georgetown were such that they did not represent strong markets for transit. In addition, there was strong citizen opposition to any further development in the neighborhood, so little potential was seen for future use. Since Metro lines were being seen as a method for channeling growth, and most stations were viewed as prime sites for high density development, a station in Georgetown would have been inconsistent with local plans for the area.

2. There was at least some citizen opposition. While many believe this was the primary reason for not building a station in Georgetown, this does not seem to be the case. This was a controversial topic in the community—some people, especially merchants, were in favor of a station. Others saw no need for one and were vocal in their concerns that it would attract outsiders and contribute to development pressures.

There is no official record showing neighborhood opposition to locating a station in Georgetown, but neither is there any indication of a proactive effort on the part of the community to have a transit station. Since the official plans never called for a station in Georgetown, there was probably no reason for any neighborhood group to go on record as opposing it. However, the prospect of having a station in the area probably would have generated some community reaction because of their well-documented interest in preventing further development.

Farragut Square station

Another question often asked is, "Why is there no connection between Farragut North and Farragut West stations?" The NCTA was interested in building another transfer station in the central business district to relieve some of the pressure that would otherwise develop at Metro Center. In the mid-1960s NCTA planners proposed building a single station at Farragut Square. It would be built, however, by cut-and-cover method, with its attendant disruption of the surface area for a significant amount of time. The National Park Service decided that disrupting the landscaped surface of the square would be undesirable. They persuaded NCTA to build two separate stations on either side of the square instead. "Knockout panels" have been built in each of the two stations to facilitate the possible construction of a 1,700-foot-long underground passageway at some future date.

October: General Manager Carmen E. Turner receives APTA's *Jesse L. Haugh Award*. The award goes annually to the transit manager "who has done the most to advance the urban transit industry in the U.S. and Canada."

1990
April 18: Metro establishes newspaper recycling program at all rail stations.

May 18 Metro awards $6.3 million contract to Cubic Western Data to upgrade 275 of the 407 farecard vendors and 100 of the 164 add-fare machines. Upgrade enables machines to accept $10 and $20 bills in addition to $1 and $5 bills.

June 21 Metro Board approves installation of pay telephones on station platforms.

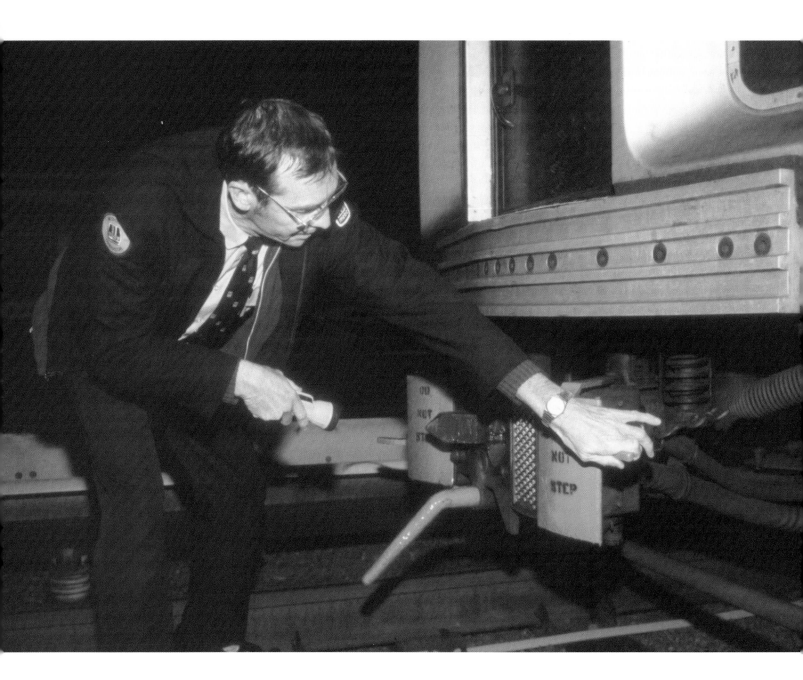

CHAPTER 3

The Long Metro Day

24 Hours in The Life of Metro

Metro never sleeps. Trains run from before 5:30 a.m. weekdays until after midnight, and until 2 a.m. on Friday and Saturday nights. Maintenance happens around the clock. Most track and train control maintenance can take place only in the small hours of the morning when the trains are not running. Metro owns a wide variety of track maintenance vehicles that are active only at night, and every passenger train receives a thorough electronic safety test nightly before being placed into service the next day.

This section focuses on the men and women who keep Metro running.

BEFORE DAWN: PREPARATION FOR REVENUE SERVICE

Putting the train into service on time is a demanding daily task for the Operations Control Center.

A train operator inspects his train in the pre-dawn hours before placing it into passenger service.

Opposite: A train operator prepares his train for passenger service in the pre-dawn hours.

A bus driver reports for work at 4:27 a.m.

TRAINS AND BUSES START TO ROLL: EARLY MORNING START OF SERVICE

A yardmaster directs train movement in Metro's Brentwood yard just north of Union Station.

Supervising yard movement is a task that requires energy and organization.

THE CRUSH: THE HEIGHT OF THE MORNING RUSH HOUR

Above: The station kiosk is a friendly place to find help and information.
Left: Advising customers is one of a Metrobus driver's most important functions. Metro is proud of its stellar customer service.

Top left: A friendly smile is an important part of Metro's customer service.
Top right: Metrobus supervisors keep things running smoothly at Anacostia station.

Bottom: Alexandria's King Street station, a busy Metrorail, Metrobus, AMTRAK and Virginia Railway Express hub, stands just east of the landmark George Washington Masonic Memorial.

Top: The Metro Orange Line on U.S. Interstate 66 in Fairfax County, Va. The passenger-carrying capacity of the two trains in the picture is about the same as that of all the cars in the traffic jam.

Bottom: Metro's new low-floor small buses serve neighborhoods more easily than standard 40-foot buses.

MIDDAY BEHIND THE SCENES: NO NAPPING AT METRO

Top: Dupont Circle station's unique circular entrance.

Bottom left: Installing a new SmarTrip target on a fare gate.

Bottom right: Metro rail cars are maintained by hundreds of highly skilled mechanics.

Left top: A Metrobus gets a new coat of paint.

Left bottom: Near Columbia Heights station on Metro's Green Line.

Top left: Maintaining Metro's facilities requires many gallons of paint.

Top right: Metro's tunnel ventilation fans keep air moving underground.

Center left: Just like on your personal automobile, the brake pads on a subway car need to be serviced frequently.

Center right: Metrorail has eight service and inspection yards and two heavy repair shops. Here a mechanic works on a track maintenance vehicle.

Bottom right: Major bus maintenance takes place at Metrobus's Bladensburg heavy repair shop.

Top left: Metro has lots of specialized equipment for things like bridge maintenance.

Top right: Metro does much of its own rail car rehabilitation work.

Center left: A "revenue" crew restocks a fare vendor.

Center right: Money counting machines at Metro's revenue collection facility.

Bottom left: An automatic fare collection technician services a fare vendor.

Top left: A back-lighted station map is a little brighter after a cleaning with glass solution.

Top right: Complex electronic gear is maintained at Metro's Brentwood rail car shop.

Center left: Metro's landscaping has won awards for design excellence. All grounds are expertly maintained.

Center right: Metro's customer information agents receive thousands of calls a day.

Bottom right: For all buses in service, the Metrobus Control Center is only a radio call away.

Top left: Bus electronics have become quite complex.

Top right: Automatic train control equipment in Metro's yards can be maintained during the day shift.

Center left: Metrobus mechanics are a highly skilled group.

Below right: Metro's Transit Police can patrol some areas best by bicycle.

Opposite top: Moving to and from Huntington station on the southern end of Metro's Yellow Line.

THE AFTERNOON SURGE AND THE EXTENDED EVENING RUSH HOUR

Top: The Grosvenor-Strathmore station on Metro's Red Line.

Bottom left: Customer information calls continue until late in the evening.

Bus drivers and supervisors work together to keep things running on time.

Above: The rapid pace at afternoon rush hour.

Left: A train operator moves out of the yard for afternoon rush hour.

Top left: A rush hour sunset at busy Silver Spring station.

Top right: The location of Grosvenor-Strathmore station on Rockville Pike at Tuckerman Lane near the intersection of U.S. Interstate 270 and the Capital Beltway encourages ample passenger traffic.

Bottom left row: Washington's many visitors rely on the friendly people at Metro to help them find their way.

LATE-NIGHT ON THE SYSTEM

AFTER MIDNIGHT: METRO NEVER SLEEPS

Top left: Installing new running rail on Metro's Main Line is night work.

Top right: Metro's mechanical shops are in operation 24 hours a day

Center left: Track maintenance is usually done at night...winter or summer, rain or shine.

Center right: Metro has eight primary bus garages and two annexes.

Lower right: Station cleaning goes on somewhere on the Metro system nearly every night.

Opposite lower left: L'Enfant Plaza station is one of Metro's downtown hubs.

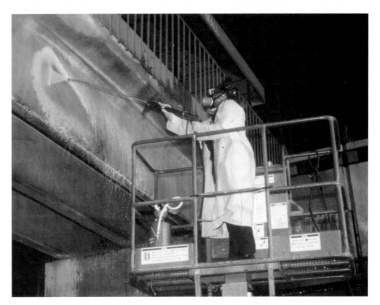

Above: The West Falls Church yard is teeming with activity all night long.
Below: Under-car equipment can be serviced only when the car is up on a lift in the shop.

Opposite top: Unpainted concrete, a part of the coffered arch station design, is cleaned frequently.
Opposite lower left: Using audio and computer tapes, Metro keeps a complete record of all train control activities.
Opposite lower right: Escalator maintenance goes on around the clock.

Customers and Communities

Metro at Your Service

etro's customers are not only its passengers, but also the communities it serves.

CUSTOMERS

With a combined rail and bus ridership averaging more than one million passenger trips per day, Metro has a unique and varied customer base that includes the citizens of the National Capital Region, employees of the federal government, students and visitors from all over the country and the world.

More than 360,000 federal employees in the National Capital Region benefit from the services of Metrorail and Metrobus. Of Metrorail's daily ridership, 36 percent are federal workers who rely on the system to make their daily commute to and from their jobs.

Approximately 23 million people visit the Washington, D.C. area each year, and many of them depend on Metrorail and Metrobus to travel around the area.

Metro is an integral part of the college and university experience in the Washington area. It also plays a vital role in providing transit services for elementary, middle school and high school students. Metro offers a reduced fare for primary and secondary school students in the District of Columbia under a program sponsored jointly with the District government. The District government reimburses Metro for the difference between the school fare and the regular fare. Metrobus tailors many routes to serve schools.

Opposite: Welcoming home Americans who were held hostage at the American embassy in Teheran, 1981.
Right: Smithsonian station, with an entrance on the National Mall, is one of the stations most frequently used by tourists.

COMMUNITIES

In addition to serving individual customers, Metro serves whole communities. From downtown to the suburbs, Metro has generated development. Forty percent of all the people entering the urban core of Washington, D.C. during a typical rush hour do so by transit. That is the second highest "mode split" in the nation, surpassed only by the New York City metropolitan area. Without a strong transit presence, much of Washington's recent downtown development would likely have gone to the suburbs.

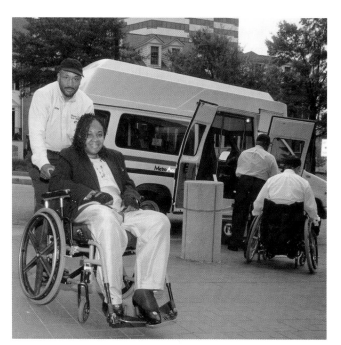

Left Top: Metro's stations are fully accessible. The fare vendors have Braille instructions for visually-impaired customers.
Left center: Returning home from Florida via Reagan National Airport and Metro.
Left bottom: School children board a Metrobus in the afternoon.

Above top: MetroAccess vans provide door-to-door service for those who cannot make use of regular Metrorail or Metrobus services.
Above center: At events such as Try Transit Week, Metro strives to attract children who will become regular transit-users later in life.

Sept 22 Red Line begins operating north of Silver Spring to Forest Glen and Wheaton stations, adding 3.2 miles to system.

October 1 Metro adds four-story garage with 1,300 spaces on north side of Vienna station.
October 2 Robert L. Miles, Metrobus operator, earns second in field of 111 in 1990 International Bus Roadeo in Houston, missing first place by one point.

October 27 Congress gives final approval to legislation providing additional $1.3 billion in federal funding over eight years for construction of rail system.

Above top and above right: Entries in the annual student poster contest. *Bottom:* 2000 Poster of the Year by Ginger Sapperstein.

Bottom: Ginger Sapperstein of the Joan Reynolds Art Studio in Derwood, Md., the winner of the 2000 student poster contest, with Keri Schrader, the reigning Miss Maryland, Metro Board Chairman Gladys Mack, and Carlton Sickles, chairman of the Board's safety committee.

1991

April 16 Wheaton station parking garage is fully opened, adding 500 parking spaces to previous 450.

May 11 First Green Line stations open—U Street-Cardozo, Shaw-Howard Univ and Mt Vernon Sq-UDC—in 1.66-mile segment north of Gallery Pl-Chinatown.

June 7 and 8 (Friday and Saturday) Desert Storm victory celebration on Mall generates two ridership records for Metrorail—highest Saturday ridership—786,300 trips, and highest weekday ridership—577,800 trips.

June 15 Blue Line opens from King Street to Van Dorn Street in Alexandria, 3.57-mile extension bringing system to 79 miles and 67 stations.

August 17–18 Metrobus maintenance team—Leonard Makowski, Eugene Medley and Kent Harrison—takes second among 34 teams in International Bus Maintenance Roadeo in Chicago.

Frequent fire and disaster drills with local fire services help keep Metro safe.

Bottom right: Frequent inspections of fire safety equipment are part of Metro's regular safety program.

SERVICE HOURS GROW AS RAIL LINES GROW
As Metrorail grew in size, it extended its service hours.

March 29, 1976 When the rail system opens it operates from 6 a.m. to 8 p.m. on weekdays and closes on weekends and federal holidays except July 4.

Sept. 25, 1978 Metrorail extends weekday service hours to midnight.

Sept. 30, 1978 Metrorail begins Saturday service from 8 a.m. to midnight and starts operating most federal holidays.

Sept. 2, 1979 Metrorail begins 10 a.m. to 6 p.m. service on Sundays.

June 29, 1986 Metrorail extends Sunday closing from 6:00 p.m. to midnight.

June 27, 1988 Metrorail begins weekday service at 5:30 a.m. instead of 6 a.m.

Nov. 5, 1999 Metrorail extends service on Friday and Saturday nights to 1 a.m.

June 30, 2000 Metrorail extends service on Friday and Saturday nights to 2 a.m. as a pilot project.

October 1 Metrobus Operator Robert Miles earns second place in International Bus Roadeo in Toronto. **October 22** U.S. Department of Transportation is first cabinet-level federal agency to join MetroPool program. MetroPool offers tax-free employer subsidy to people who commute by Metrobus or Metrorail.

December 19 Metro Board approves financial plan that sets schedule and funding for *Fast Track* program for finishing 103-mile Metrorail system by 2001. *Fast Track* allows Metro to build remaining 13.5 miles earlier and within $2.07 billion approved by Congress and local governments.

December 28 Metrorail opens 2.88-mile Green Line segment serving Waterfront, Navy Yard and Anacostia stations.

Top: Bethesda looking north at the intersection of Wisconsin Avenue and Old Georgetown Road—October 1974.
Center: Friendship Heights looking north—October 1974.

Top: Bethesda looking north at the intersection of Wisconsin Avenue and Old Georgetown Road—March 12, 1997.
Center: Friendship Heights looking east—March 12, 1996.

At suburban locations such as Silver Spring and Bethesda in Montgomery County, Md., and at Ballston in Arlington, Va., Metro's presence has spurred a major building boom, as can be seen in these before and after photos.

Metro's ability to raise property values and attract development is now proven and understood by the community, and efforts are underway to put that quality to good use. The New York Avenue in-fill station planned for the Red Line

is expected to be the magnet for redevelopment of the New York Avenue corridor in the northeast sector of the city.

The Authority has been an industry leader in "joint development" of its property to maximize its return on investment to the community. Numerous private developments connect directly to Metro stations. At many downtown locations, the Metro entrance is beneath the corner of a commercial building.

1992
April 26 Metrorail begins earlier Sunday hours, opening at 8 a.m. instead of 10 a.m.

August 1 Local neighbors join Northern Division in celebrating garage's conversion from turn-of-the-century trolley barn to modern bus garage.

1993
January 20 Metrorail sets new ridership record, 811,000 trips, during President Clinton's Inauguration Day.

February 2 Metro launches Metrochek, voucher system that allows participants to redeem Metro fares for service on 29 Washington-area transit systems. Metrochek is available through MetroPool program.

Top: Silver Spring facing north—January 1976.
Center: Ballston looking east—January 1979.
Bottom: Ballston looking west—January 1979

Top: Silver Spring facing northwest—March 27, 1998.
Center: Ballston looking east—September 30, 1993. Rosslyn and Washington in background at the top of the photo.
Bottom: Ballston looking west—September 30, 1993.

SPECIAL EVENTS

Metro routinely provides service for extraordinary crowds drawn to the Nation's Capital for special events such as festivals, marches, presidential inaugurations, sporting events and political demonstrations. No other transit system in the country is called upon to serve these types of events as frequently.

Top left: Throughout its history, Metro has been serving customers attending political demonstrations. The March on Washington, August 27, 1983.

Top right: Independence Day fireworks on the Monument Grounds...one of Metro's busiest evenings of the year. Metro moves about one-quarter million people between 10 p.m. and midnight following the fireworks display.

Center left: Families use Metro on their way to celebrate the arrival of the new millennium, December 31, 1999.

Center right: Metro works cooperatively with the Susan B. Komen Breast Cancer Foundation to support the Race for the Cure event in the Nation's Capital each summer.

Bottom left: A Metrobus in an inaugural parade.

METRO AS A CROWD PLEASER

Metro's at its best moving large crowds in a short time. Here are some events that set ridership records for their time.

Feb. 3, 1988 Washingtonians welcome the Redskins home from the Super Bowl victory with a parade. Metro carries 564,265 riders.

April 29, 1988 Washington for Jesus celebration attracts 565,000 riders to Metrorail.

Jan. 20, 1989 Metrorail carries 604,000 passengers during the inauguration of President Bush.

June 7 and 8, 1991 Desert Storm victory celebration on the National Mall generates two ridership records for Metrorail—highest ridership on a Saturday (786,300) and highest weekday ridership (577,800).

Jan. 20, 1993 Metrorail carries 811,000 riders during President Clinton's inauguration, the highest single day ridership to date.

Oct. 16, 1995 The *Million Man March* yields the second highest single day ridership in Metro's history, with 804,145 passenger trips.

March 4 EPA holds press conference at newly renovated Northern Division announcing latest clean air standards for bus exhaust. Metro announces plan to buy 600 buses with cleaner-burning engines.
May 10 Metrobus earns APTA's *Most Improved Safety Award* for transit systems in North America.

August 28 Metrobus maintenance team takes second in APTA's International Maintenance Roadeo in Denver. Team includes Leonard Makowski, Eugene Medley and Kent Harrison.
October 5: Metrobus Operator Robert Miles ranks third in APTA International Bus Roadeo in New Orleans.

December 11 Metrorail begins service on 7.96-mile Green Line segment that includes West Hyattsville, Prince George's Plaza, College Park-U of Md and Greenbelt stations. It connects with Red Line at Fort Totten. This completes 89.5 miles of the 103-mile system.

THE INFORMATION AGE: WWW.WMATA.COM AND WWW.METROOPENSDOORS.COM

Metro joined the information revolution in 1996 when its Internet site went online. At the site, customers can get not only firsthand information on the state of Metro service, they can also purchase fare cards and passes including SmarTrip cards.

The Ride Guide is a unique interactive trip planning tool included in the Metro Web site. The customer simply selects the origin, destination and time of departure or arrival; The Ride Guide provides the best route, including Metrorail, Metrobus and bus services operated by the local governments in the transit zone. For origin and destination, the user can submit an address, intersection, landmark or tourist attraction. The Ride Guide is widely recognized as a superlative tool for planning transit travel in and around the Nation's Capital.

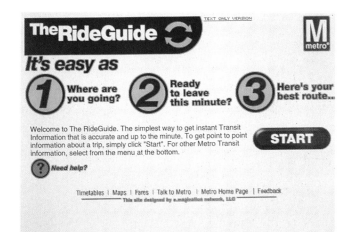

The Ride Guide, Metro's interactive trip planning software, is available online at Metro's Web site—www.metroopensdoors.com. or www.wmata.com.

Metro's home page at www.metroopensdoors.com or www.wmata.com.

December 31 Metro completes its safest year of heavy construction. Injury rate, 0.8, is fraction of industry average, 5.8. One sprained ankle and two pulled shoulders were only injuries during 794,000 hours of Metro construction in 1993.

1994
May 3 Metro Station Manager Steven Morrison receives *Gold Award for Hospitality* from Washington, D.C. Convention and Visitors Association.

May 16 Metro begins *MetroAccess*—curb-to-curb service for people whose impairments keep them from using Metrorail, Metrobus or fixed-route local bus service. Metrobus receives top safety award, APTA's *Alan S. Boyd Silver Award*, for its low accident rate and innovative safety program.

CHAPTER 5

Metro Behind the Scenes

Evolution and Revolution

Metro has continuously been evolving. Over the last 30 years construction methods and materials have improved considerably, and the explosive development of computers and electronic technology has revolutionized the transit industry.

THE LEADING EDGE IN TUNNEL CONSTRUCTION

Since Metro broke ground in December 1969, tunneling techniques have developed more than they did in the preceding two millennia. For many years explosives were used to blast rock to create a tunnel. At first black powder was used, but by the mid-19th century the preferred charge was dynamite.

By the early 20th century, various tunnel boring machines were tried with gradually improving success. The move toward the use of tunnel boring machines was prompted in part by the danger inherent in the use of explosives.

The conventional drill-and-blast method could tunnel through about 100 feet of rock in a good week. As tunnel boring machines have improved, the advance of 1,000 feet per week or more is no longer newsworthy.

Opposite: "Shotcrete" on the tunnel walls.

Right: An early tunnel-boring machine—the "jumbo drill rig"—hard at work.

Evolving Excavation and Construction Methods

At the time Metro's first solid rock station was built at Dupont Circle, heavy steel beams had to be installed every 18 inches to keep the rock load from collapsing. Later, as the Red Line progressed out Connecticut Avenue NW and Wisconsin Avenue in Bethesda, Md., advances in the art of mining favored the excavation of two smaller circular tunnels, one for each track instead of one large tunnel that would contain both tracks. This permitted the costly steel ribs to be replaced by "shotcrete," a quick-drying concrete that is hosed onto tunnel walls under high pressure directly behind the tunnel boring machines. The same methods were used to build the Orange Line between Rosslyn and Ballston in Virginia.

1995
February 6 Metro begins smart-card technology demonstration with its GO CARD program at 19 Metrorail stations, five parking lots and three Metrobus lines.
May 15 Metro and Montgomery County open *Kidstop,* the first child care center at a Metrorail station, at Shady Grove.

May 22 Metrorail carries two billionth rider.
June 6 Prototype of *American Ikarus,* Metrobus' newest articulated bus, debuts at White House. President Clinton and Hungarian Prime Minister Gyula Horn give it a tour. Bus is American-Hungarian joint venture.

June 22 Joseph Alexander, Metro's longest-serving Virginia representative on the Board of Directors, retires from the Board after more than 24 years of service.

By the time Wheaton and Forest Glen stations were built, computers were used to analyze rock loads, and the New Austrian Tunneling Method permitted an egg shaped tunnel to be excavated that would make a natural, self-supporting rock arch. With most of the load being borne by the rock itself, a simple concrete lining could be installed.

Excavation through soft, wet materials has changed even more impressively. At the time of Metro's first construction, a soft earth tunneling machine known as a "sand-hog" was used. The machine used a shield resembling a huge tin can with both ends removed. As the shield rotated and moved forward, a mechanical claw inside the shield scooped out material and fed it to a conveyor belt that moved it farther back for disposal. Workers moved along behind the machine to reinforce and line the resulting tunnel.

Metro pioneered the use of a special "earth pressure balance" tunneling machine to build the Green Line tunnels almost 100 feet beneath the Anacostia River. Ordinarily when crews tunneled deep beneath a river, they used a shield to hold back the watery sand material through which they were digging. It was necessary to pump compressed air into the digging area to help hold back the in-rushing material. People working in such a compressed air environment tended to develop nitrogen sickness or "the bends," a painful and potentially deadly condition more commonly associated with diving.

In contrast to the compressed air shield, the earth pressure balance machine uses a compartment immediately behind the digging face that contains a slurry to hold back in-rushing wet sand. This permits the excavation crews to work in normal air pressure, thereby greatly reducing their risk of injury.

The Yellow Line segment that crosses the Washington Channel near East Potomac Park was built using a sunken tube. Large, drum-like metal structures were fabricated in

Opposite: The last tunnel on the 103-mile system. This photo shows the "hole through" at the Congress Heights station. The tunnel boring machine is on the other side of the wall. Only its face with the cutting surface is shown here.
Opposite: Forest Glen station under construction.

Dupont Circle station under construction.

September 27 Metro unveils passes/farecard vendors at Metro Center. The machines dispense passes and multiple fare cards, accept and update GO CARDS and use synthesized voice to guide sight-impaired through steps in using machine. Metro schedules installation of the machines on all station mezzanines over several years.

October 16 *Million Man March* yields second highest ridership in Metro's history—804,000 trips. Highest ridership day remains January 20, 1993 inauguration of President Clinton.
November 3 Metrobus carries its three billionth rider.

1996
March 28 and 29: Some 500 experts in planning, architecture, engineering, development, financing and federal policy-making gather for first Metro-sponsored *Symposium for Transit-Oriented Development and Livable Communities.*

a plant on the Susquehanna River and floated to the site, then carefully sunk to a dredged trench in the channel bed. The sunken structure was then covered with soil and rocks to protect it from ships passing overhead.

Ground Water Control

In addition to evolving methods of tunnel excavation, the design of underground structures has also changed dramatically since Metro first began to build. At some stations along the Red Line under Connecticut Avenue NW one can stand quietly and hear the sound of cascading water running behind the vaulted arch of the station. At some stations one can see evidence that the tunnel liner has been pierced many times to inject waterproofing material to stop leaks that damage equipment and cause unsightly stains.

By contrast, a visit to one of the newest stations, such as Wheaton or Columbia Heights, reveals a bone-dry interior. These dry conditions are the result of a "raincoat" of PVC and drainage material that has been applied to the back of the tunnel liner. Metro was the first in the U.S. to use this ground water control technique which is now the worldwide standard for tunnel construction.

Floating Slabs

WMATA was also the first transit system in the nation to use cushioned track slabs to reduce noise and vibration. In Metro's tunnels and on its elevated structures, the rails are attached to steel-reinforced concrete slabs. Unless protected in some way, trains riding over these structures will be noisy and uncomfortable because of vibrations, and over time could be harmful to the structure itself and surrounding buildings. To mitigate these effects, Metro has installed thick neoprene pads to act as shock absorbers beneath the concrete slabs.

March 29 Metro celebrates 20 years of providing efficient, reliable transit.
May 9 Metro Board approves purchase of 262 new Metrobuses.

1997
January 1 Commuter rail riders from Maryland and Virginia can buy monthly pass that offers unlimited MARC-Metrorail or VRE-Metrorail travel. It is part of one-year demonstration program.

January 10 Metro conducts *Regional Mobility Investment Conference* as call to action for region to develop mobility plan for 21st century.

January 27 Green Line Shortcut begins as six-month experiment. Passengers during peak periods can ride between Greenbelt on Green Line and Farragut North on Red Line without transferring. Later, shortcut is continued because of its success in drawing new riders.

Top: The Yellow Line tunnel tube set afloat on the Susquehanna River for its trip to Washington. *Bottom:* The Yellow Line tunnel tube being sunk to its place on the bed of the Washington Channel.

Opposite: Tunnel construction nears completion at Foggy Bottom-GWU station in the summer of 1975.

February 27 Metro Board adopts Blue Line extension into the Adopted Regional System contingent on the successful completion of the Final Environmental Impact Statement and a financing plan. The three-mile extension from Addison Road to Largo Town Center includes an intermediate station at Summerfield.

April 1 Maryland General Assembly budgets $4.7 million in fiscal 1998 for preliminary engineering and environmental impact study on extension of Blue Line by three miles and two stations to Largo Town Center.

June 7 Race for the Cure is first beneficiary of new Metro policy to open early, on request, to support large community events. Sponsoring organization pays hourly rate to Metro and is reimbursed from revenues collected.

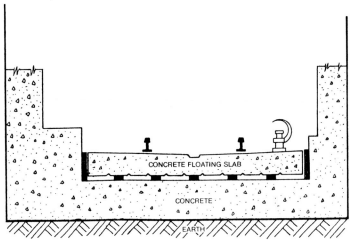

Above: Applying the PVC "raincoat."

Left: Floating slab diagram.

Right: Workers assemble a tunnel boring machine in preparation for Green Line work north of Mt. Vernon Sq/7th St-Convention Center station.

June 26 Metro Board approves White Flint East, Metro's largest joint development project to date. To be phased in over 11 years, the 32.42-acre project includes 1.2-million square feet of office space, 100,000 square feet of retail space and 1,338 residences.

June 29 Service begins to Franconia-Springfield, adding 3.3 miles to Blue Line and increasing Metrorail to 75-station, 92.4-mile system.

September 11 Station Manager Tyrone Jefferson Sr. wins the *1997 Capital Star Award,* the Washington, D.C. Convention and Visitors Association's highest award for a front line employee.

Stacked Tunnels

The original proposed alignment of the Green Line north of Columbia Heights station incorporated a split tunnel. The outbound section was under Park Road and the inbound tunnel was under Monroe Street. Along Monroe Street, the inbound tunnel passed directly underneath the historic Tivoli Theater and many residential properties. To overcome community objection to taking the property and to improve community response to Metro construction, the Authority rerouted the inbound tunnel, "stacking" it directly under the outbound tunnel along Park Road. The stacked tunnel configuration significantly minimized disruption to the community. It is the only bored stacked tunnel arrangement in the Metrorail system and one of the few among the transit properties in the United States. The use of this innovative technique saved many residents' homes including 32 properties along Monroe Street.

THE EVOLUTION OF OPERATIONS CONTROL CENTER TECHNOLOGY

The bus and streetcar systems in Washington always had a central point from which vehicle movements could be monitored and controlled. The Metro system is no exception. The main difference is that the Metro automatic train control

September 23 American Public Transit Association awards Metro its *Outstanding Achievement Award*.
October 4: Metrorail registers fourth highest ridership, 725,900 trips, during *Promise Keepers* assembly on National Mall. System opens at 4 a.m.

October 9 Metro Board approves recommendations of Regional Mobility Panel (see January 10) to plan, fund and operate Metrobus in manner similar to Metrorail.

November 16 Metro opens new Gallery Pl-Chinatown entrance on northeast corner of 7th and F streets NW in alcove of MCI Center, which opens December 2.

Top left: DC Transit streetcar control center.

Center left: Operations Control Center in 1975.

Lower left: Operations Control Center in 1982.

Top right: In 1991, Operations Control Center system displays were a series of CRT monitors.

Center right: The Operations Control Center passenger operations desk in 1993.

Opposite:

Top: Operations Control Center in 1998 after installation of the system display at the front of the room.

Center: Operations Control Center in 1991.

Bottom: Control of Metrobus operations will improve in the coming years as automated vehicle tracking systems are installed. For now, control is maintained through constant radio contact.

1998

February 20 Metro celebrates the 25th anniversary of Metrobus with 25-cent bus fares all day, a photo exhibit at the Capitol and free rides on *The Silver Anniversary Bus*.

May 15 Metrobus Operator Robert L. Miles recognized for operating two million accident-free miles.

July 6 Metro begins its first assignment as outside contractor for bus service and maintenance. Under contract to the Potomac and Rappahannock Transit Commission, Metro runs and maintains 53 buses and 22 smaller vehicles for OmniRide and OmniLink service in Prince William County, Va.

(ATC) system is linked to a computer and display monitors in the operations control center. The ATC system displays the actual position of each train at all times and enables supervisors in the control center to manipulate the signals, switches, traction power system and tunnel ventilation fans.

The original Metro control room was state of the art for that era. As the system has grown so has the central control requirement, and the control room has evolved along with the computer and electronics industry. The difference is evident from these photos.

METRO'S EVOLVING FARE COLLECTION TECHNOLOGY

From the beginning, Metro planned to use the latest fare collection technology. It purchased a system that used a paper card with a magnetic stripe for encoded stored value. Metro's state of the art automatic fare collection system is familiar to most Washingtonians and to many people who have visited the Nation's Capital over the years. Many people will remember that the system was not ready for service on opening day in 1976. Exact change fare boxes—the type found on buses—were installed in the Metro stations instead. In fact, it was not until July 1, 1977, 15 months later, that the automatic fare collection system went into service and the fare boxes were removed.

At first the fare collection system had a lot of difficulties. The equipment was prone to malfunction, and Metro engineers struggled for years to improve its performance.

In the early days of Metro operation, the Authority doubted that the fare collection system would be able to accommodate heavier than normal demand. Consequently, during special events such as the annual Independence Day celebration on the Mall for which large crowds were expected, Metro turned the system off and collected exact fares in barrels instead.

As the electronics industry developed better hardware, Metro took advantage of the latest in designs. Solid state components have replaced the moving parts that were most problematic, and the automatic fare collection system has gone from being one of Metro's weakest features to one of its most successful.

In 1999 Metro introduced its latest fare collection innovation: SmarTrip cards. The size and shape of a plastic credit card, a SmarTrip card has a computer chip that can

Top left: Metro's paper farecard with magnetic stripe.
Center left: Bus-type fareboxes were the heart of Metrorail's fare collection system for the first 15 months of operation.
Bottom left: Riders insert farecards in faregates as they enter and leave. Fares, which vary by length and time of day of the trip, are detected upon exit.
Center right: Barrels are used on July 4th to collect fares.

Opposite left: Metro's SmarTrip cards are used for Metro fares and parking.
Opposite right: Machines in stations sell farecards and passes, and add funds to SmarTrip cards.

March 1 Metro begins selling fares, passes and merchandise online. Customers use Visa, MasterCard or Discover at *www.wmata.com* and receive their purchase by mail in five days.

May 18 Metro launches *SmarTrip*, the permanent, rechargeable plastic farecard that is good for Metrorail trips and Metro parking.

June 20 Metro launches fare simplification for Metrobus riders. The new system offers a single fare, $1.10, to ride any regular route Metrobus at any time of day; a free transfer between buses; and a 25-cent transfer from Metrorail. Express route riders pay $2. The program also introduces an all-day Metrobus pass for $2.50.

be programmed with up to $180 in fare value. It is permanent like a credit card, rather than expendable like a regular farecard. If lost, it can be cancelled and replaced without monetary loss to the customer. In some cases the SmarTrip card doubles as a bank card and credit card. These cards accept value not only at Metro's fare vendors but also at the automatic teller machines of the issuing bank. It is even possible to add value to the SmarTrip card using the Metro Internet site. Under a program called SmartBenefits, employers can put value onto their employees' SmarTrip cards as an employment benefit.

In use, the card is touched to a target on the fare vendor or fare gate to activate the equipment. It can even be used to pay for parking at Metro's parking lots and garages.

It never leaves the customer's hand and is immune to most of the remaining few malfunctions that characterize regular fare cards. It has brought about an enormous improvement in customer service, and customers have responded by purchasing SmarTrip cards in far greater quantities than were originally expected. It truly has been one of Metro's greatest success stories.

June 23 Mayor Anthony A. Williams announces a financing plan for a New York Avenue station on the Red Line between Union Station and Rhode Island Ave station.

September 7 Metro begins operating five new Ride On routes under contract with Montgomery County.

September 18 Metro begins revenue service on the mid-city Green Line segment that includes Columbia Heights and Georgia Ave-Petworth stations in northwest Washington. Green Line Shortcut eliminated.

November 5 Metrorail extends hours to 1 a.m. Friday and Saturday nights as part of an eight-month experiment.

CHAPTER 6

Infrastructure Renewal

Preserving the Metro Investment

Metro completed the 103-mile system in January 2001 with the opening of the final segment of the Green Line. Consequently there is a perception that the system is "new," especially when compared with similar operations in Boston, New York and Chicago. In reality, older sections of Metrorail are something of a Dorian Gray: their nearly pristine appearance masks the rigors of use over the past 25 years. In 1999 Metro contracted for a comprehensive assessment of the condition of the Metrorail and Metrobus system. That study concluded that Metro's aging physical assets need increasing reinvestment beyond routine maintenance to keep them in good repair. In response, the Authority has embarked on a 25-year, $9.8 billion program to renovate its oldest structural facilities and replace equipment that has reached the end of its useful life.

Requisite renewal of Metro entails the repair, rehabilitation or replacement of virtually every element of this huge and complicated system:

- Trains and buses
- Stations
- Maintenance and operating facilities
- The trackway, tunnels and bridges
- Power and propulsion systems
- Communications systems
- Computer systems

This massive undertaking is proceeding to protect the public's investment in the Metro system. System renewal means providing for more efficient operations by keeping Metro state of the art.

While much of the work is behind the scenes, customers will see refurbished stations and parking lots, enhanced signage and information sources, canopies over escalators exposed to the elements, and, of greatest import for a growing system, more buses and trains and rehabilitation of the existing fleet.

Opposite: Rehabilitating a Metro rail car is months'-long process. *Right:* Pressure cleaning overnight keeps station entrances looking attractive during the day.

New rail cars have different interior colors from the rest of the fleet. Older cars will be changing to the new color scheme as they are renovated.

Delegate Eleanor Holmes Norton speaks at the unveiling of the prototype 5000 series Metrorail car delivered by the AAI/CAF consortium, February 3, 2000.

NEW RAIL CARS

The new cars are being manufactured by a partnership of two companies: AAI Corp. of Baltimore, Md. and Construcciones y Auxiliar de Ferrocarriles (Rail Car Builders) of Madrid, Spain. Metro has ordered 192 cars, each costing $1,560,000.

The interior colors of the new cars differ from the orange, cream and brown of the Rohr and Breda fleet. Seats are upholstered in a combination of three colors called Potomac Blue, Chesapeake Sand and Colonial Burgundy. The carpets have a tweed pattern of those colors. The interior of the older cars will be changed to the new color scheme as the cars are renovated over the next few years.

The new cars also have electronic signs in the passenger compartment that display the name of the next station, the color of the line on which the train is operating and the side of the car on which the doors will open at the next stop. This sign is especially helpful to those who have difficulty hearing announcements made by the train operator over the PA system.

Two new safety features have been included:

1. Barriers have been placed between each pair of cars to help vision-impaired customers recognize the difference between that space and an open door and prevent them from stepping between the cars thinking they are boarding the train.

2. The new cars also have an extra panel attached to the sill of each passenger door. The panel narrows the gap between the sill and the granite edge of the station platforms, making it less likely that a person's foot can be caught between the car and the platform.

BUSES FOR THE FUTURE

Heavy Overhaul

After about seven and a half years of service a Metrobus has traveled about 325,000 miles, and an increasing effort is necessary to sustain its performance at an acceptable level. By 12 years of age, many of the bus's critical parts have worn out, and the vehicle reaches the end of its useful life. However, if the bus is restored to like-new condition at the seven-and-a-half year point, it can continue to operate for another seven and a half years, thereby extending its total useful life to 15 years.

In 1994 WMATA established a bus overhaul program to rehabilitate bus mechanical and electrical systems, replace interior upholstery and repaint the exterior. This

2000
January 1 Metro's long preparation for the Y2K roll-over pays off with an uneventful day carrying passengers to and from the millennium celebrations on the Mall and elsewhere. Metrorail hours are extended to 3 a.m. The 21.5-hour day, which begins 5:30 a.m. December 31, generates 415,000 rail trips. As a precaution against Y2K glitches, Metro stages 300 buses near rail stations and stops all trains at station platforms for a five-minute pause before and after midnight.

January 25-26 Metrorail keeps operating as major snowstorm shuts down federal government, all schools and most businesses for two days.

January 31 Metro moves customer service operations to its new call center near Silver Spring station.

A wheelchair customer uses the ramp on one of Metro's new low-floor buses.

Metro's bus overhaul program is a leader in the transit industry.

rehabilitation also permits the incorporation of new technology and safety enhancements and keeps the fleet in compliance with air quality requirements.

The overhaul program reduces the capital outlay for new buses. A new bus costs about $300,000. The cost to overhaul a transit bus is $97,000.

Low Floor Buses

In April 2000, Metro received the first of 100 low-floor buses. By reducing the height of the floor and eliminating the entry steps, these vehicles need no wheelchair lift. An extending entry ramp is used instead.

Compressed Natural Gas Buses

After much study, the Metro Board of Directors concluded that it would be beneficial to include a number of vehicles powered by compressed natural gas (CNG). Compressed natural gas is thought to be cleaner than diesel fuel and better for the area's air quality. In December 2000 the Board approved the purchase of 100 CNG buses in lieu of diesel and the installation of a CNG fueling facility at the Bladensburg Division.

February 4 Director of the U.S. Office of Management and Budget announces $25 million for the New York Avenue station in the proposed fiscal 2001 federal budget. The sum matches the $25 million committed separately by the city and the business community.
Same day: U.S. DOT Secretary Rodney Slater pledges $259 million in federal funds to build the extension of the Blue Line from Addison Road to Largo, Md. Governor Parris Glendening had already pledged $175 million as the state's share for the project.

February 10 Metro Board approves purchase of former Hechinger Distribution Center in Landover, Md. as a multipurpose Metro building. The property is Metro's largest, with 647,000 square feet of floor space on 28 acres of land at 2500 Pennsy Drive, directly opposite Landover Metrobus Division.

CHAPTER 7

Building the Future

The WMATA Transit Service Expansion

Plan—A Blueprint for the Next Generation

The visionary men and women who pioneered the Metro system saw clearly that the National Capital Region would continue to grow. This world capital is now the keystone of an emerging global community in a new millennium. It is unlikely, however, that anyone in the 1960s foresaw the pace and extent of growth that has transformed the Nation's Capital into a dynamic metropolitan area of more than 4.5 million people. It is not only the home of the federal government, but has also become a center for burgeoning high tech industries undreamed of 40 years ago.

GROWING TO MEET THE NEEDS OF AN EXPANDING REGION

The Authority's *Transit Service Expansion Plan*, adopted in April 1999, is composed of a series of bold regional initiatives formulated with considerable involvement of state and local governments, regional agencies and private organizations in the Washington area. It is the first effort to direct future extensions of Metrorail since the original plan to build the 103-mile Adopted Regional System. The plan embraces the objectives of the region's Vision Plan over the next quarter century, focusing in particular on the following three goals:

Doubling Ridership
The region must commit to double transit ridership by 2025 to maintain transit's existing market share; to enhance its contribution to mobility and accessibility, improved air quality and reduced traffic congestion; and to accommodate increased regional growth and travel demands.

Linking Activity Centers for Economic Health
Major transportation corridors and the regional transportation system must include a significant transit element to complement the road and bridge system. Transit must connect major commercial, retail, entertainment and residential activity centers and other transportation facilities in a way that ensures that the region remains economically viable and competitive.

Improving Livability and Quality of Life
Public transportation must be envisioned as an essential means to support and enhance community livability and quality of life.

Four Elements of the Expansion Plan
The expansion plan comprises four elements as follows:

1. *Improving Metrorail Accessibility:* Improve Metrorail accessibility and capacity by expanding parking, feeder bus services and remote Park & Ride lots, improving pedestrian and bicycle facilities, acquiring additional rolling stock and increasing the ability of the core of the Metrorail system to accommodate future ridership growth.

2. *Improving bus service and expanding it into new areas:* Metrobus service and local bus services have not kept up with local population growth which has doubled since 1960. Bus expansions should focus on several markets, including suburb-to-suburb, reverse commuting to suburban employment centers, access-to-job initiatives (promoted at the federal, state and local level) and better service in the core areas. A network of express bus service and strategically located commuter parking lots is needed to take advantage of the new High Occupancy Vehicle (HOV) lanes being planned for several

Prince George's Plaza station on Metro's Green Line has a massive parking structure located directly above the station.

Groundbreaking for the New York Avenue station. *From left:* Metro general manager Richard A. White; Dr. I. King Jordan, president of Gallaudet University; Therman Walker of the North Capital Business Association; Dr. Marc Weiss; D.C. City Councilman Vincent Orange; Delegate Eleanor Holmes Norton; D.C. Mayor Anthony Williams; Metro Board member Gladys Mack; D.C. City Councilman and Metro Board member David Catania.

major roads. This will help move people quickly with attractive, comfortable buses and using creative service concepts such as Bus Rapid Transit.

3. *Adding Metro Stations, Entrances and Capacity to the Existing System:* Ground already has been broken for the New York Avenue in-fill station on the Red Line, and a new entrance is being built in the Mt Vernon Sq/7th St-Convention Center station to link directly to the new convention center. Plans also are being formulated for new entrances at Crystal City, Rosslyn and Ballston.

4. *Expanding Fixed Guideway Systems by Half:* Metro is studying other fixed guideway systems—light rail, other rail technologies and busways. The goal is to provide for at least a 50 percent mileage expansion over the next 25 years which amounts to 50 to 60 additional miles.

STRETCHING CORE CAPACITY

If Metrorail ridership doubles in the next 25 years, can Metro's 29 busiest stations and connecting lines handle the increased demand? That question is at the center of the *Core Capacity Study* that is scheduled for completion in

early 2002. The study is designed to answer two very important questions:

- Can the core of the Metrorail system, as presently configured, sustain current ridership volumes and accommodate future ridership increases at an acceptable level of performance? If not, what must be done?
- Can the presently configured core sustain the increased passenger demand generated from future expansions? If not, what must be done?

This is one of the most comprehensive reviews undertaken by any transit system in the United States.

NEW YORK AVENUE STATION: A NEW STOP. A NEW START.

With bands playing and pennants flying, people thronged to the groundbreaking of New York Avenue station on Saturday, December 16, 2000. The turning of the earth for the first "in-fill" station came less than a month before completion of the 103-mile Metrorail system and the opening of the Green Line in Prince George's County, Md.

As with past Metro stations, New York Avenue station is at the core of a revitalization initiative. In this case, it's the redevelopment of Washington's New York Avenue corridor that is expected to emerge as a prime site for high tech companies, federal agencies and retail activity. The development plan for the new station comprises three funding partners: the District of Columbia, the federal government and private interests. Creation of this unique funding arrangement was spearheaded by a stakeholder group known as the New York Avenue Metro Station Corporation under the leadership of Dr. Marc Weiss, a District of Columbia public policy specialist.

By using the design-build contracting method, Metro expects to compress construction time to less than four years, awarding the contract in mid-2001 and opening by the end of 2004, depending on funding.

The $84 million station is being built on the west side of the existing Red Line between Florida Avenue and M Street NE. It will have two entrances, one at Florida Avenue and another at M Street. After it begins operating, the existing Red Line tracks will be used for car storage.

July 1 Metrorail extends hours until 2 a.m. Friday and Saturday nights as a one-year experiment.
July 31 Average weekday ridership for July hits record 616,233 making it the highest daily ridership month in Metro's history.

September First order of 100 full-size, low-floor buses enters service.
September 14 SmartBenefits, a Web-based program that allows an employer to load the Metrochek benefit directly into an employee's *SmarTrip* card, is launched with a ceremony at L'Enfant Plaza.

October 2 Federal executive order becomes effective requiring that all federal agencies make full Metrochek benefits ($65 per month) available to all federal employees in the region.

K AVENUE STATION
TUAL DRAWING - PLATFORM VIEW

K AVENUE STATION
UAL DRAWING - PAVILLION VIEW

K AVENUE STATION
TUAL DRAWING - NW AERIAL

Funding for construction is being shared equally among the District of Columbia, the federal government and the private sector. Private sector funds are to be raised through a special assessment district proposed to be established around the station. D.C. Mayor Anthony Williams identified the station as one of the critical projects for the District in mid-1999, and the District provided the initial $5 million for Metro to begin the preliminary engineering and environmental clearances on the new station. Initial daily ridership at New York Avenue station is projected at 6,600, with 10,000 using it daily by 2020.

THE LARGO EXTENSION: THE FIRST EXTENSION BEYOND THE 103-MILE ADOPTED REGIONAL SYSTEM

Expected to open in 2004, the 3.2-mile, two-station, $434-million extension of the Blue Line to Largo Town Center with an intermediate station at Summerfield achieves a number of "firsts" in Metrorail history.

- It is the first segment to be added to the 103-mile, 83-station Adopted Regional System, bringing the total to 106 miles and 85 stations.

- It is the first of the four *legs* in Prince George's County to extend beyond the Capital Beltway.

SUMMERFIELD STATION
CONCEPTUAL DRAWING - ENTRANCE VIEW

October 16 Metrorail has its third highest ridership day as a result of the Million Family March. The Metrorail tally was 688,467 passenger trips.

October 26 Metro Board adds New York Avenue station to the Adopted Regional System.

October 28 Metro Board expands Transit Zone to include Charles County, Md.
December 16 Ground is broken for the New York Avenue in-fill station.

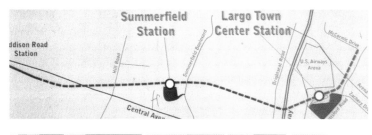

SUMMERFIELD STATION
CONCEPTUAL DRAWING - MEZZANINE VIEW

LARGO TOWN CENTER STATION
CONCEPTUAL DRAWING - ENTRANCE VIEW

An architect's rendering of the proposed Silver Spring Transit Center.

WMATA worked with local communities as well as state, local and federal agencies to select an alignment that maximizes the effectiveness of the extension while minimizing its impact on surrounding areas. The alignment of the segment was developed to blend into the surrounding area with at-grade, open-cut, elevated and underground segments.

THE SILVER SPRING TRANSIT CENTER

The Silver Spring Transit Center, still in the early stages of design and approvals, is an initiative of Montgomery County and the state of Maryland that centers around the relocation of the Silver Spring MARC station to the Metro station site. A direct connection between MARC and Metro is envisioned. The Transit Center is expected to be a multi-level building housing an improved local transit and long-distance bus terminal, Kiss & Ride spaces and commuter-oriented retail service businesses.

DULLES CORRIDOR PROJECT: FROM WEST FALLS CHURCH TO LOUDOUN COUNTY

The Dulles Corridor Rapid Transit Project is developing a phased rapid transit service for the 24-mile corridor, with service primarily in the median of the Dulles Airport Access Road, extending from a point near West Falls Church station on the Orange Line to Dulles Airport and beyond. The Dulles corridor is undergoing rapid growth in both households and jobs. Tysons Corner, Reston, Herndon and eastern Loudoun County are major employment centers with millions of square feet of new office space and millions more under construction or in the planning stages. Dulles International Airport is the fastest-growing airport in the world.

The project will consist of a phased implementation of improved public transit services. The initial phase of express bus service was established by Fairfax County in 1999. A bus rapid transit service is expected to begin operation in 2003. Metrorail is currently scheduled to begin service to Tysons Corner by 2006 and to Dulles Airport by 2010, depending on the flow of federal funds to the project.

Now the project has moved into the environmental impact statement (EIS), preliminary engineering and financial plan phase. The EIS is being prepared by a project

2001
January 13 With the 6.5-mile extension of the Green Line from Anacostia to Branch Avenue, Metro opens the last five stations in the 103-mile Adopted Regional System.

Metrorail Alternative

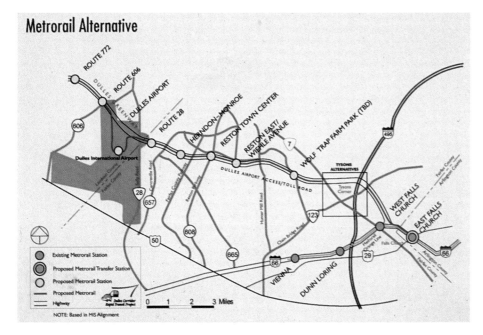

The Orange Line to Centreville

A major investment study conducted by the Virginia Department of Rail and Public Transportation in 1999 recommended the extension of Metrorail from Vienna/Fairfax-GMU station to Centreville, Va. The Commonwealth of Virginia is now initiating the preparation of an environmental impact statement on highway and transit improvements to Interstate 66.

Light Rail

After a nearly 40-year absence, streetcars may once again appear on the streets of the National Capital Region. The District of Columbia has asked Metro to do a preliminary evaluation of nine routes that would be candidates for light rail transit.

For years, Maryland has promoted double-duty for the Georgetown Branch "rail-to-trail" to serve also as a corridor for light rail transit connecting Silver Spring and Bethesda. This proposal would provide a convenient link between the two legs of the Red Line.

Virginia is considering two light rail lines, both tying in with Metrorail and Metrobus at the Pentagon. One would connect the Pentagon with Bailey's Crossroads via Columbia Pike, and the other would link the Pentagon to Braddock Road station via Crystal City.

team that includes Metro, the Virginia Department of Rail and Public Transportation and the Federal Transit Administration. Metro is the recipient of federal funds for this work; a total of $42 million has been appropriated to date. The approved 2001 federal budget provides an additional $50 million for the project.

OTHER PROJECTS

In addition to the projects currently on the drawing board, Metro and its state and local partners have imagined other unique ways to serve the growing travel demand of the National Capital Region.

The Purple Line

At the direction of Maryland and Virginia, Metro is working on project development for two segments of what has popularly become known as the "Purple Line." One proposal would connect the New Carrollton area in Prince George's County to a location near Montgomery Mall in Bethesda. The other would connect southern Prince George's County to Alexandria and the Metro Blue Line. The key to this is the provision of dedicated transit lanes on the new Woodrow Wilson bridge.

Expanded Parking

Expanding Metro's people-moving capacity, among other things, means expanding parking capacity at stations. Today, many Metro parking lots are filled before the end of the morning rush hour.

The new 2,200-space garage that opened in January 2001 at Vienna/Fairfax-GMU station is the prototype of a structure that will net almost 8,400 additional parking spaces when identical structures are built at other Metro stations.

February 11 Cleatus E. Barnett is the longest-serving member of the Metro Board of Directors. He has represented Montgomery County, Md. on the Metro Board for over 30 continuous years from February 11, 1971 to the present.

March 27 Metro celebrates the 25th anniversary of the start of service.

Every day, people just like you step through our doors to go to work, to school, to shop, to travel, to play and to fulfill their hopes and dreams. From the bus, to the rail, you can get to where you really want to be. Find out what doors Metro can open for you. Call 202.637.7000 or visit www.metroopensdoors.com to check out our Ride Guide for trip planning.

Metro Opens Doors

For the more than two billion residents and visitors who have boarded a train over the past quarter of a century, the Metro system has provided a fundamental requirement of American metropolitan life: mobility. The familiar "doors opening" announcement has been a portal for millions to the abundant opportunities provided by the National Capital Region in jobs and career advancement, education, recreation, shopping and the ability to participate actively in the region's rich cultural and entertainment offerings. The system has become so popular that, among U.S. transit properties, it is now second only to New York City in number of riders.

Over its first 25 years, Metro has aggressively pursued a customer focus to make the system easier and more pleasant to use. More recent customer enhancements have included:

- A simplified fare system with seamless transferring between buses and trains and other transit services in the region.
- State of the art fare and parking payment with the SmarTrip card.
- Use of credit and debit cards to purchase fares and passes.

- Introduction of special passes to serve the travel needs of students, visitors and conventioneers.
- Audio bus stop announcements on buses and electronic signs on trains to display the next station.
- Electronic signs in stations to keep customers informed about train arrivals and other vital information.
- A regional Customer Call Center that provides personalized trip planning, faxed bus and rail schedules, and e-mail services.
- A dynamic Web site—featuring The Ride Guide—a comprehensive, interactive travel planning service—and real-time information about service, elevator and escalator status, weather advisories and the best way to ride Metro to the region's many special events.

By providing safe, reliable transit service, Metro's 9,000-plus employees play a crucial role in keeping this increasingly congested region moving. Over the next 25 years, the accent on customer service will continue to produce improved conveniences. This strategic combination of reliable transit service and customer convenience represents Metro's commitment to ensuring that "America's Transit System" continues to open its doors to the next generation of riders pursuing their lives and aspirations in the unique and vibrant National Capital Region.

Opposite: Metro's proven ability to "open doors" to communities and to provide opportunities for the people who live there is a natural theme for an advertising campaign. The campaign includes newspaper ads like this one, as well as television and radio commercials.

Appendix

METRO BOARD OF DIRECTORS AND INDIVIDUAL DATES OF SERVICE

Name	Representing	Service Dates	Name	Representing	Service Dates
Alexander, Joseph	Virginia	1/14/71–6/22/95	LaPlaca, Raymond G.	Maryland	4/10/80–3/11/82
Aluisi, Francis J.	Maryland	10/20/67–12/13/68	Lowe, Schuyler	District of Columbia	2/20/67–6/30/67
Anderson, Stanley J.	District of Columbia	12/3/70–12/30/71	Mack, Gladys W.	District of Columbia	3/1/79 -6/27/91
		3/23/72–8/2/73			4/27/95–
Babson, Frederick A.	Virginia	2/20/67–12/24/69	Mann, Frank E.	Virginia	9/9/76–6/28/79
Back, Kenneth	District of Columbia	6/16/67–11/3/67	Marburger, John H.	Maryland	2/20/67–10/16/67
Barnett, Cleatus E.	Maryland	2/11/71–	Mason, Hilda H. M.	District of Columbia	1/18/79–12/31/98
Beatley, Charles E., Jr.	Virginia	7/16/70–5/4/72	Mathe, Robert E.	District of Columbia	2/20/67–11/3/67
		3/7/74–6/24/76	McConchie, H. Winfield	Virginia	5/11/72–1/17/74
		7/19/79–9/15/83	Miller, Woodrow W.	Maryland	3/25/82–2/9/84
Berger, Ernest J.	Virginia	2/9/95–12/14/95	Milliken, John G.	Virginia	1/13/83–1/10/85
Birely, Avis	Maryland	10/8/70–2/4/71	Moore, Jerry A., Jr.	District of Columbia	4/17/69–3/12/72
Bozman, Ellen M.	Virginia	1/9/86–1/14/88			9/20/73–12/31/84
		1/18/96–12/18/97	Munsey, Everard	Virginia	1/9/75–12/30/75
Burcham, John B., Jr.	Maryland	1/7/71–6/14/73	Nevius, John A.	District of Columbia	8/17/72–12/19/74
Calhoun, Robert L.	Virginia	6/13/85–6/30/88	Nophlin, Calvin	District of Columbia	10/14/99–
Casey, Donald C.	Virginia	10/13/83–4/25/85	Ostrom, Robert B.	Maryland	2/23/84–1/3/91
Castaldi, Richard J.	Maryland	1/6/83–1/3/91	Pemberton, Hilda R.	Maryland	1/17/91–10/27/94
Casto, Harold J.	Virginia	2/20/67–10/20/67	Phillips, A. Leslie	Virginia	1/9/70–1/7/71
Catania, David A.	District of Columbia	1/14/99–	Phillips, Rufus	Virginia	1/9/75–12/18/75
Christeller, Norman L.	Maryland	1/9/75–10/7/76	Prentiss, Louis W., Jr.	District of Columbia	7/3/67–11/3/67
Clark, James E., III	District of Columbia	10/30/80–2/12/81	Price, Deborah A.	District of Columbia	6/12/92–5/11/95
Coates, James E.	District of Columbia	1/9/75–1/13/77	Rachal, Anthony M. III	District of Columbia	10/25/91–4/27/95
Colasanto, Nicholas A.	Virginia	2/20/67–7/9/70	Reynolds, Tom H.	District of Columbia	2/20/67–6/30/67
Cropp, Linda W.	District of Columbia	1/17/91–1/14/93	Rhoads, Lee M.	Virginia	2/20/67–1/7/71
Davey, John P.	Maryland	1/17/91–	Ricks, Jay E.	Virginia	1/5/68–12/27/68
Downs, Thomas M.	District of Columbia	5/14/81–5/12/83			1/14/71–10/21/71
Duncan, Kenneth V.	Maryland	4/5/79–2/28/80	Rivers, David E.	District of Columbia	2/5/87–5/21/87
Euille, William A.	Virginia	7/13/00–	Robinson, Henry S., Jr.	District of Columbia	8/17/72–12/19/74
Evans, Jack	District of Columbia	2/11/93–12/31/98	Schneider, Douglas N. Jr.	District of Columbia	1/13/77–8/14/80
Falck, Nancy K.	Virginia	2/14/85–12/10/87	Scott, James M.	Virginia	2/25/82–1/10/85
Fauntroy, Walter E.	District of Columbia	11/9/67–2/27/69	Shackleton, Polly	District of Columbia	11/9/67–12/24/69
Fisher, Joseph L.	Virginia	12/2/71–12/19/74	Shacochis, John P.	Virginia	1/16/76–12/20/79
Fletcher, Thomas W.	District of Columbia	12/7/67–10/16/69	Sickles, Carlton R.	Maryland	2/20/67- 4/26/73
Francois, Francis B.	Maryland	3/23/78–10/16/80			1/9/75–3/16/78
Frankland, Walter L.	Virginia	1/4/79–1/3/80			9/10/81–
Garrott, Idamae	Maryland	3/30/72–12/19/74	Smith, Frank, Jr.	District of Columbia	1/10/85–1/3/91
Gilpin, C. Bernard	District of Columbia	11/7/85–11/20/86	Spellman, Gladys Noon	Maryland	12/27/68–12/31/70
Gleason, James P.	Maryland	2/20/67–8/27/70	Thomas, Ned R.	Virginia	1/10/69–12/24/69
Graham, Jim	District of Columbia	1/14/99–	Ticer, Patricia S.	Virginia	7/28/94–12/14/95
Grotos, Dorothy T.	Virginia	1/10/80–1/6/83	Tobriner, Walter N.	District of Columbia	2/20/67–10/27/67
Gullett, William W.	Maryland	6/21/73–12/19/74	Travesky, Marie B.	Virginia	1/10/80–2/11/82
Hanley, Katherine K.	Virginia	1/21/88–2/9/95	Trotter, Decatur W.	Maryland	3/11/99–
		1/22/98–	Tucker, Sterling	District of Columbia	9/20/73–1/19/78
Hardy, Willie J.	District of Columbia	2/16/78–1/18/79	Walker, Lois L.	Virginia	1/18/96–5/11/00
Harris, Herbert E.	Virginia	1/15/70–12/19/74	Washington, Walter E.	District of Columbia	1/9/75–3/1/79
Hartlove, David G., Jr.	Maryland	10/30/80–12/16/82	Watson, Matthew S.	District of Columbia	1/21/88–1/23/92
Haywood, Margaret A.	District of Columbia	1/9/70–7/13/72	Watt, Graham	District of Columbia	1/9/70–2/24/73
Hovsepian, Dickran Y.	Maryland	2/11/71–6/3/71	Whipple, Mary Margaret	Virginia	1/24/85–1/9/86
Hussman, William H.	Maryland	8/12/71–3/16/72			1/21/88–12/14/95
Hyland, Gerald W.	Virginia	7/13/95–1/8/98	White, Francis W.	Maryland	6/21/73–3/16/78
Jackson, T. Michael	Virginia	7/28/88–6/23/94	Wholey, Joseph S.	Virginia	2/5/76–12/21/78
Johnson, William B.	District of Columbia	2/14/85–2/28/85	Willard, Henry K, II	District of Columbia	1/6/72–6/22/72
Jones, Horace G.	District of Columbia	7/14/83–11/8/84	Wilson, Robert W.	Maryland	3/23/78–12/15/78
Kauffman, Dana	Virginia	1/18/96–	Wineland, F. Kirwan (Kirk)	Maryland	10/27/94–1/28/99
Kinlow, Eugene	District of Columbia	5/11/95–11/5/98	Yeldell, Joseph	District of Columbia	11/9/67–11/20/70
Kramer, Rose C.	Maryland	2/20/67–2/4/71	Zimmerman, Christopher E.	Virginia	1/22/98–
		1/27/77–8/27/81			

MEMBERS OF METRO'S "SHADOW" BOARD OF DIRECTORS
October 1966 to February 20, 1967

Name	Representing
General Charles Duke	District of Columbia
Walter N. Tobriner	District of Columbia
Robert E. Mathe	District of Columbia
Tom Reynolds	District of Columbia
Schuyler Lowe	District of Columbia
James Gleason	Maryland
Frank Lastner	Maryland
Carlton R. Sickles	Maryland
Rose Kramer	Maryland
John Marburger	Maryland
Robert Burkart	Maryland
Gladys Noon Spellman	Maryland
Leo Urbanske	Virginia
Lee M. Rhoads	Virginia
Frederick A. Babson	Virginia
Harold Casto	Virginia
Nicholas Colasanto	Virginia

METRO'S GENERAL MANAGERS
Pre-WMATA

1961-1965 C. Darwin Stolzenbach, NCTA Administrator
1965-1967 Walter J. McCarter, NCTA Administrator

WMATA General Managers

February 1967 to February 1976	Jackson Graham
February 1976 to November 1976	Warren D. Quenstedt (Acting)
November 1976 to May 1979	Theodore C. Lutz
May 1979 to May 1983	Richard S. Page
May 1983 to December 1990	Carmen E. Turner
December 1990 to March 1991	William A. Boleyn (Acting)
March 1991 to March 1994	David L. Gunn
March 1994 to March 1996	Larry G. Reuter
March 1996 to August 1996	Robert Polk (Acting)
August 1996 to present	Richard A. White

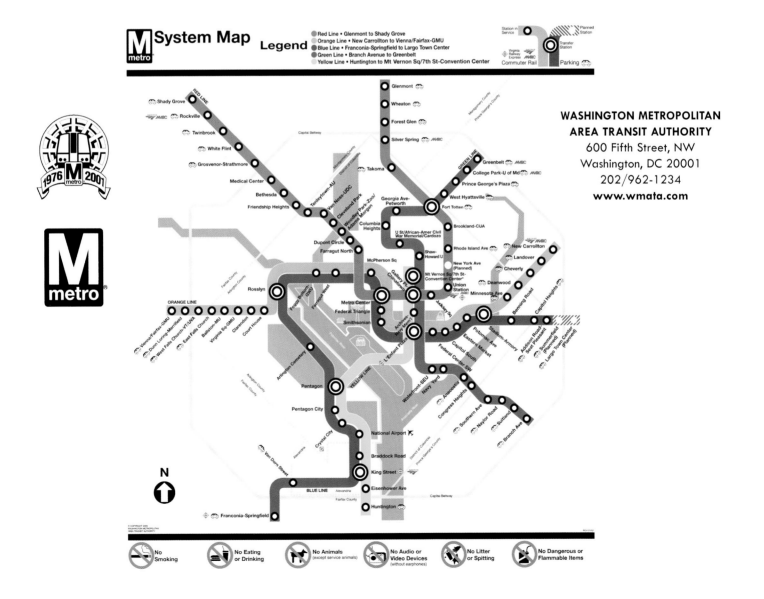

**WASHINGTON METROPOLITAN
AREA TRANSIT AUTHORITY**
600 Fifth Street, NW
Washington, DC 20001
202/962-1234
www.wmata.com

Index

Illustrations are indicated by page references in **boldface** type.